REMARKABLE FAITH

"When we're at our wit's end, drained of every ounce of spiritual energy, REMARKABLE FAITH invites us to reach out—just one more time—to our loving Father who delights in saving us. Keep this book handy for those times when it seems all hope is lost...for that is the moment unfailing faith connects us to a never-failing God."

—Maisie Sparks, author of
Holy Shakespeare! 101 Scriptures That Appear in Shakespeare's Plays, Poems, and Sonnets

"In REMARKABLE FAITH, Shauna Letellier has accomplished no easy feat—she reawakens our sense of surprise with the word of God and welcomes us into a fresh freedom in our faith in Jesus. She is a noteworthy new voice who surely has more books to come, and I'll be waiting for the next!"

—Cindy Lambert, co-author of
One Light Still Shines

"Shauna Letellier delves into the stories of Jesus' healings with fresh perspectives and windows of insight. Her conviction of the power of Scripture and faith in the Christ provide hope and encouragement. Intriguing us with sanctified imagination, we find a realistic and true-to-life engagement with those who met Jesus—not only as they invite and inspire us, but also as they challenge us to go deeper in our faith."

—Gregory C. Carlson, PhD, Chair and
Professor of Christian Ministries and
Leadership, Trinity International University

"Like a tour guide sharing her beloved hometown, Shauna Letellier leads you through the winding back streets of eight of Jesus' miracles. Her delightful blend of storytelling, research, and commentary will make you weep, wonder, and wander ever deeper into the Word. As it explores the unexpected faith of ordinary people, REMARKABLE FAITH awakens a longing for the same relentless pursuit of Jesus—the Strength in your weakness, the Fulfillment of your needs, the one true Lover of your soul."

—Kathi Lipp & Cheri Gregory, co-authors of
*Overwhelmed: How to Quiet the Chaos
and Restore Your Sanity*

REMARKABLE FAITH

WHEN JESUS MARVELED AT THE FAITH OF UNREMARKABLE PEOPLE

SHAUNA LETELLIER

Faith
Words

New York Nashville

FaithWords
Hachette Book Group
1290 Avenue of the Americas, New York, NY 10104
faithwords.com
twitter.com/faithwords

First Edition: July 2017

FaithWords is a division of Hachette Book Group, Inc. The FaithWords name and logo are trademarks of Hachette Book Group, Inc.

The publisher is not responsible for websites (or their content) that are not owned by the publisher.

The Hachette Speakers Bureau provides a wide range of authors for speaking events. To find out more, go to www.hachettespeakersbureau.com or call (866) 376-6591.

Unless otherwise noted Scripture quotations are taken from the Holy Bible, New International Version®, NIV®. Copyright © 1973, 1978, 1984, 2011 by Biblica, Inc.™ Used by permission of Zondervan. All rights reserved worldwide. www.zondervan.com The "NIV" and "New International Version" are trademarks registered in the United States Patent and Trademark Office by Biblica, Inc.™

Scripture quotations marked (esv) are taken from The Holy Bible, English Standard Version® (ESV®), copyright © 2001 by Crossway, a publishing ministry of Good News Publishers. Used by permission. All rights reserved.

Scriptures noted amp are taken from the Amplified® Bible. Copyright © 1954, 1962, 1965, 1987 by The Lockman Foundation. Used by permission.

Library of Congress Cataloging-in-Publication Data has been applied for.

ISBNs: 978-1-4555-7168-0 (paperback), 978-1-4555-7169-7 (ebook)

Printed in the United States of America

LSC-C

10 9 8 7 6 5 4 3 2 1

*For Zach, Spencer, and Levi, my gifts from
God who have pointed me toward my blessed
desperation for my Savior.*

*For Kurt, my "man of few words," your
encouragement and patient support have enabled
and fueled my writing. Your straightforward,
hilarious editorial remarks have kept me honest.*

*For Jesus, whose kindness led me to the
gift of repentance. Who allowed me to try and
fail hard so that I would be eager to receive his rescuing
grace. Thank you for tenderly teaching me you notice
faith even in unremarkable people like me.*

Because the people God uses don't have to know a lot of things, or have a lot of things—they just have to need him a lot.

—Sally Lloyd-Jones, *The Jesus Storybook Bible*

Contents

Finding Faith

God is looking for broken men who have judged
themselves in the light of the cross of Christ.
When He wants anything done, He takes up men
who have come to the end of themselves, whose
confidence is not in themselves, but in God.

—H. A. Ironside, "Men God Wants"

Maybe you've resolved, again, to study your Bible
more, serve at your church, or be a better wife, mom,
husband, father, employee, or Christian. But the daily
montage of your life accuses you of weak faith. Your
life bears no evidence of ark-building, sea-crossing
acts of faith. After a long day, week, or season you
find yourself collapsed in your chair, shaking your
head. Maybe you've just tucked your sweethearts

into bed. With enthusiasm you've read to them of a giant-slaying boy with great faith in God. Perhaps you flipped through the rest of the children's Bible, looking for a character with whom you can identify.

Or, maybe you've just stepped off the treadmill after your morning exercise, and driving to the same places, dealing with the same people, and doing it all again makes you feel like you're still on it. One foot in front of the other, the belt whirrs round the axles, day after day. Something about your daily life doesn't seem congruent with faith that pleases God.

But you are wrong.

When we look for examples of great faith in the gospels, we think of the disciples. They sat with rapt attention on the side of a mountain listening to Jesus teach with authority about a higher standard of righteousness. When he told them not to worry about where clothes and food would come from, he referred to these disciples who had left jobs, businesses, and family to follow him as "you of little faith" (Matthew 6:30).

We might think of Peter, who took a leap of faith to walk on water to Jesus. But when Peter lost sight of who Jesus was and focused on the raging storm around him, he began to doubt and drown. Then

Jesus said, to the only disciple with the courage to leap, "You of little faith..., why did you doubt?" (Matthew 14:31).

We might think of the disciples going through the towns of Galilee following in Jesus' footsteps and attempting to do as he had done. At the foot of a mountain, nine of them were attempting to free a little boy from a torturous demon. They could not. When Jesus arrived, what did he have to say to his disciples? "Thank you for attempting to do my work in my absence"? No. Instead, he scolded their misplaced faith: "You unbelieving and perverse generation, how long shall I stay with you?" Jesus drove out the demon and freed the boy. Embarrassed and confounded, the disciples asked, "Why couldn't we drive it out?" He said to them, "Because you have so little faith" (see Matthew 17:14–20).

If Jesus found so little faith with his disciples, whom he chose, did he find faith at all? Yes, he did.

Sprinkled throughout the gospels are the stories of eight nameless examples of faith. We identify them not by their names, but by their afflictions. Their lives were marked by desperation, pain, fatigue, hopelessness, disability, poverty, loneliness, and sin.

Each of them sought Jesus in unabashed desperation.

With nothing to offer and nothing to lose, they went to great lengths to get to him. Some crawled through the dust. Some interrupted important gatherings. Others were relegated to roadsides and caves so they screamed for his help as he passed by.

What did Jesus notice about them? Their affliction? Their social impropriety? Perhaps. But the thing he remarked about, even marveled at, was their faith.

Yes, Jesus found faith. Remarkable faith. But in the most unremarkable people. These are their stories.

It's been said that a picture is worth a thousand words, but when it comes to describing Jesus, it is easier to use a thousand words to paint a mental picture. I suspect that's one reason the gospels are filled with stories.

We can say Jesus was compassionate, but something more comprehensive is portrayed when we see him kneeling in the dirt by a crumpled boy, helping him to his feet, and giving him back to his father (see Luke 9:42). When we read that, we have a clearer glimpse of what Christ's compassion might mean.

In the words of Philip Yancey, "It is one thing to talk in abstract terms about the infinite boundless love of God. It is quite another to tell of a man who lays down his life for his friends..."[1]

In the biblical vignettes in this book, I have taken the challenge issued by Bible professor Howard Hendricks to read the Bible imaginatively and pray this prayer: "Lord, clothe the facts with fascination. Help me crawl into the skin of these people—to see through their eyes, to feel with their fingers, to understand with their hearts, and to know with their minds."[2] The characters' backstories, motivations, and the various ways they came to hear about Jesus are plucked from my imagination. Each fictional retelling, however, is based on the true and inspired stories recounted for us through the Holy Spirit by the writers of Scripture (see 2 Peter 1:12).

I have tried to stay close to the Scriptures with these retellings. Where parallel passages were different, I combined the words and accounts of the gospel writers into one. Where Scripture was unclear on motives, I imagined one I felt was reasonable in the situation. Where Scripture was silent, I sifted through possibilities presented in a variety of Bible commentaries. Then I wove a little historical, geographic, political, religious, and cultural context together to drape the fabric of fiction over the framework of Scripture. The more I studied the stories, the more I learned about Jesus. I am fascinated, and he is magnified.

I am tempted to say studying these stories has brought the Bible to life for me, but that would be inaccurate. It was not the Bible that needed to be brought to life. God's word is already living and active (see Hebrews 4:12). It is my mind and imagination that had been dulled and deadened, whether by overfamiliarity or distraction. Perhaps my imaginative look at these stories will begin to awaken your mind to what God has given in his living and active word.

My prayer is that through these reimagined stories the Holy Spirit will stir or reignite in you a real affection for Jesus Christ. Not only is he worthy of worship, service, and time, he is worthy of love.

Weak Faith

The Father of a Demon-Possessed Boy

A man in the crowd answered, "Teacher, I brought you my son, who is possessed by a spirit that has robbed him of speech. Whenever it seizes him, it throws him to the ground. He foams at the mouth, gnashes his teeth and becomes rigid. I asked your disciples to drive out the spirit, but they could not."

"You unbelieving generation," Jesus replied, "how long shall I stay with you? How long shall I put up with you? Bring the boy to me."

So they brought him. When the spirit saw Jesus, it immediately threw the boy into a convulsion. He fell to the ground and rolled around, foaming at the mouth.

Jesus asked the boy's father, "How long has he been like this?"

"From childhood," he answered. "It has often thrown him into fire or water to kill him. But if you can do anything, take pity on us and help us."

" 'If you can'?" said Jesus. "Everything is possible for one who believes."

Immediately the boy's father exclaimed, "I do believe; help me overcome my unbelief!"

When Jesus saw that a crowd was running to the scene, he rebuked the impure spirit. "You deaf and mute spirit," he said, "I command you, come out of him and never enter him again."

The spirit shrieked, convulsed him violently and came out. The boy looked so much like a corpse that many said, "He's dead." But Jesus took him by the hand and lifted him to his feet, and he stood up.

—Mark 9:17–27

Parallel Passages: Matthew 17:14–21;

Luke 9:37–43

Morning had come too soon. Outside, water jars clanked together and goats bawled for breakfast. The racket coaxed him from sleep. He lifted his head and glanced at his only child on the mat next to him. The arc of the boy's ribs showed through his soiled shirt as his chest rose and fell. He still smelled of singed hair and smoke.

The father counted his own heartbeats until his boy's chest rose again. Six beats between breaths. Two beats. Ten beats and still no breath. He reached over to shake his son's shoulder. Finally the boy's chest rose again. He whispered an exhale but did not wake.

Relieved, the father lay back on his bed, exhausted. He was thankful for breath and sleep and wished for more of both. Once again, last night had been appalling.

This morning, with sunlight streaming through the eastern window, he rolled from his mat and knelt to examine the sleeping boy's leg. It was blistered and blackened, muddied with blood and ash. His son was too agitated last night for him to clean it. He knew he'd have to wait until morning. He'd learned it was always best to wait until morning.

He dipped a linen cloth into the basin and squeezed it out over the burn. Cool water trickled into the wound and dissolved the bloodied ash. His son flinched. The father stopped for a moment to see if he would wake. He didn't. So the father began again. The burn needed a fierce scrubbing, he could tell. This morning he was too tired to restrain his son in order to do it. Instead, he continued to wet and wring and gently wipe.

Finally, the father poured thin wine over a clean cloth and swabbed the burn. The boy winced, but settled. By the time his father had maneuvered the boy's leg to wrap it in linen bandages, he finally woke.

He studied his son's face for signs of irritation. The boy breathed steadily, but inside his chest was a rattling that never produced a cough. Since he never spoke or startled at noises, his hollow eyes were the tunnel from which the first signals of his convulsions came. This morning, his father saw none of those signs, just a blank stare and shallow breathing through cracked lips.

"Today we are going out," he said, knowing full well he wasn't heard. He raised him to sitting and poured a little water in his mouth. The son tugged at the fresh bandage, and his father held out the cup for his son to hold, to occupy his hands and distract him without upsetting him.

Lacing his scarred and skeletal fingers through the cup's handle, he sipped.

The child was wasting away. His body was fragile and his head misshapen from the swelling of repeated trauma. His father feared the next convulsion might be the last. He knew he must go today. He'd heard of a man. Some said he was a teacher, some said a prophet of old. Others claimed he was John the Baptist come back to life. Rumors he barely hoped to believe declared that Jesus of Nazareth was the long-awaited Messiah. Whatever—whoever Jesus was, fame preceded him, followed by a wake of discarded crutches, vacant sickbeds, and throngs of happily bewildered people. Though he hadn't seen any of it himself, the father desperately wanted it all to be true.

He folded cheese and bread into a cloth, tucked it into his belt, and looked back at his son. He was still holding the cup, but the water had spilled down his chest. Better to hold the cup and spill the water than to ruin the bandage, he thought.

Sometimes the father's touch would calm the boy, and sometimes it would set him off. Which would it be today? He offered his hand to help his son stand, and the boy willingly took hold. Relief washed over the father. He smiled, grabbed his son's cloak, and led his boy out the door.

Outside of town and into the foothills they followed the village murmurings to where Jesus might be. He kept his son within arm's reach while they walked, to support his fragile frame or restrain his wildness, whichever was needed.

Perhaps Jesus had healed the sick. He strained to rein in his expectations. *My son isn't just sick!* His son required something greater than wine, oil, and linen. Neighbors, friends, and family were long past calling him "sick." After years of witnessing his violent episodes, they called him a lunatic. He was. Both mind and body were in the clutches of the devil.

His boy was a home to a demon.

Over the years the demon had repeatedly thrown his son into fires. More times than he wanted to remember, the smell of burning flesh assaulted his senses as he wrestled him from a fire. Each time, new burns blistered and old burns reopened where tender, new skin had finally grown. His wounds, always soiled with ash and dirt, required a thorough washing. Each time the scarring was worse.

His boy was getting bigger. Hardly heavier, but longer, harder to restrain, and faster to sink when the demon threw him into water. The father had lost track of the times he'd plunged himself, fully clothed, into the water to bring his writhing son up for air. He'd often been pulled under himself by the thrashing.

Without fail the two of them would emerge from the water to a crowd of onlookers, mouths agape.

Neighborhood families had grown accustomed to the recurring spectacle, but never comfortable with it. Warned by the boy's devilish shriek, families whipped around and rushed away. Mothers covered the eyes and ears of their children as his own child was slammed to the ground to flail in the mud created by his own body. Deep parental agony clawed at his heart as they fled from him and his boy.

The sight of a milling crowd jolted him back to the reason for their journey. His heart beat faster. He must be here!

Nearing the crowd, he was surprised to find an argument in progress. Local religious leaders squabbled with nine adamant strangers claiming to be Jesus' disciples. He scoured the crowd for the one called Jesus. He saw no one being healed. No one seemed to be in charge.

A woman caressing a bundle of linen shouldered her way out of the group. "Is Jesus of Nazareth up there?" he asked as she came close. Her face was pale, strained with grief, and her eyes were wet with tears. She shook her head. As she passed, he saw the sweaty little head of a shivering baby cocooned in layers of blankets.

Reluctantly, he took his son by the hand and wove his way through the crowd. Some mocked the religious leaders; others insulted the disciples. Interested and curious bystanders craned their necks to see the leaders debate. He pushed through until he was at the center of the argument. With his mangled son in their midst, they finally hushed. At the sight of his scarred flesh the religious leaders recoiled.

Suddenly it didn't seem so crowded. He studied the men. Their horrified expressions and disgusted whispers dizzied him. Desperation surfaced and the father begged the disciples, "Please…please help. Can you get rid of this evil?" With nervous anticipation he urged his son forward and waited.

Confidently, the disciples spoke—first in Aramaic, then in Hebrew, then in a more commanding tone. "Come out of him!" His son stood before them unaffected—ears still deaf, mouth still mute, eyes still sunken and vacant.

Silence mocked the disciples and vindicated the religious leaders. Finally, the religious leaders filled the silence with insults. "What made you think you could drive it out?" the leaders scolded. They forgot the boy and went on attacking one another. The mumbling of the disappointed crowd absorbed the quarrel, and they began to peel away in ones and twos.

Perhaps he'd been wrong to hope at all. *Am I a fool?*

He studied his son's face for the rapid blinking, the quivering lips, the stiffness that started in his jaw, all certain signs that the demon was about to seize him again, but the signs that normally alarmed him were absent. He pulled his son to the frayed edges of the dispersing crowd, feeling as disappointed as the mother he'd seen on the way in.

Suddenly, someone behind them shouted, "It's Jesus!" Folks came back together in a roaring swell of movement and noise. Jesus was the reason he had come. He took his son's hand again, and together they limped and budged through the onlookers toward four more men who had just joined the quarrel.

"What are you arguing about with them?" he heard one ask. *That must be Jesus.*

Before the disciples could recount the weary dispute, the father thrust himself toward Jesus in answer to the hanging question. It was his only chance.

With his hands trembling and voice shaking, above the clamor he hollered, "Teacher!" He dropped to his knees under the weight of urgency and cried,

"Lord...have mercy on us! Please, hurry. Help us!" Desperate to compact years of suffering into one precious moment, he detailed their plight.

"Teacher, I brought my only child. I beg you. Take a look at him. He suffers terribly. An evil spirit seizes him, and suddenly he'll just shriek. It slams him to the ground over and over. He foams at the mouth, grinds his teeth, and his body becomes rigid. It robs him of speech, and only with great difficulty does it ever leave him!"

He paused to catch his breath, and looked behind him to check on his son standing a few steps away.

"Today I brought him to you, but you were gone. So I begged your disciples to heal him, and they couldn't." Breathless from pouring out the litany of demonic manifestations, he waited, feeling foolishly hopeful.

"Bring him to me," Jesus replied.

Brushing dirt from his knees and tears from his eyes he turned his smudged face toward his boy. Although he was becoming agitated, the boy heeded his father's beckoning gesture.

As soon as the demon saw Jesus, the boy opened his mouth and looked into the sky. His guttural scream pierced the crowd. It was the feral and familiar warning the father dreaded. The demon slammed the boy to the ground with a sickening thud. Arms and legs flailing, muscles contracting, he rolled in the gravel. Foaming saliva dripped from his chin and muddied his face. The father's horrid description came to life.

The crowd receded. Children cried. Men threatened to restrain him, and the religious leaders stood back in horror.

The father jumped out of the way of his thrashing son, but stayed near enough to chase him if he ran toward the nearest well or stream. He skittered around to protect him from the violence foisted on him by the demon—to soften the blows by throwing his cloak under the boy's head for a moment, and to kick the largest rocks out of the way.

"How long has this been happening to him?" Jesus asked.

"From early childhood," he answered, "and it has often thrown him into fires and water to destroy him." He choked on his emotion and pointed to his convulsing son. "If you can do anything... have compassion and rescue us!"

The father was panting. The thrashing had stopped. His son lay rigid and shivering. It was too soon to touch him. To cover or clean him would only aggravate the demon and reignite the attack.

Jesus placed a weathered hand on the father's shoulder and repeated, "'If you can'?" Jesus questioned him. "All things are possible for the one who believes."

The father nodded and hung his head. He had voiced his hope but betrayed his doubt. Affirming and confessing in the same breath he exclaimed, "I believe...help my unbelief!"

When Jesus saw more people running toward them to view the spectacle, he wasted no time. With indignation and authority Jesus commanded the demon, "You deaf and mute spirit, I command you! Get out of him and never enter him again!" In unwilling obedience to its authority, the demon convulsed the boy with more violence than the father had ever seen. The boy's head was being scraped bald by repeated blows to the ground, and gravel lodged in the gashes. The demonic mauling stirred up the dust, and when it had lifted and drifted away, the boy lay in a limp, contorted heap, so much like a corpse they thought he was dead.

The boy's chest was curved underneath him. His backbones punctured his skin where they had been scratched raw against the ground. A lifetime of scrubbing, saving, and cautiously caring for a volatile child had mangled them both. Had it been for nothing? The father saw no movement or breathing, and he began to weep.

Jesus stepped toward the boy. He rolled him onto his back, and with the sleeve of his own cloak Jesus wiped saliva and soil from the boy's face. The boy blinked. His chest heaved with a gasp, and his skin flushed with color. His father stared, breathless and waiting.

Jesus took the boy's skinned and filthy hands in his own, then helped him stand. Together they took a few steps toward the father, and Jesus held out the boy's hands for the father to hold.

In the habit of studying his son before touching him, he hesitated. As he looked, he saw no trace of the demonic host he had brought to Jesus. His son blinked normally. He looked up at a flock of gulls heard squawking overhead.

He whispered, "Papa."

The father stared at Jesus, then fell to his knees again. Eye to eye with his boy, he wept and hugged him, and for the first time in years, his boy hugged him back.

The Faith No One Wants

No one wants to be the example of weak faith. Yet, at some time or another, many of us find ourselves nursing an injured faith, hoping for mercy.

This man did not meet Jesus with a load of certainty. He wanted to believe Jesus was who he claimed to be. He hoped all those stories were true, because he needed a story like that. He needed a Savior like that, but years of trauma inevitably wear a person down. Doubt feeds on a thousand dashed hopes. Remedies recommended by family, physicians, and spiritual leaders had all failed.

Perhaps he meant to manufacture some confidence on his way to find Jesus. He saw firsthand what strong conviction looked like when the piety of the religious leaders bumped into the passion of the errant disciples. What we see on display in this father is the opposite. He came dragging years of disappointment, prodded along by the countdown of a little life about to expire.

He didn't offer Jesus a prescription to fill, as if he had it all figured out. He came without suggestions and asked for mercy. Spiritually rattled, he bared the truth of his shattered spirit.

Jesus was not offended by the father's weakness. After Jesus drove out the demon and rescued the boy, the crowd was no longer gasping about the horrors of demonization, nor at the weakness of faith. They were amazed at the greatness of God (see Luke 9:43).

The Embarrassing Prayer of Weakness

We despise the trials of broken bodies, impossible dreams, and unspeakable tragedy. Suffering drives us to Christ for help when we can do nothing else. Under spiritual strain, we beg him to help, and wonder if he can do anything at all. It's not how we like to envision ourselves coming to Jesus. It seems like remarkable faith ought to stand tall, with its fist firmly pumped toward heaven, proclaiming, "I believe!" But Jesus sees through manufactured confidence, and the façade of made-up faith.

Remarkable faith is the braided strands of doubt, hope, and wonder at a God who is able to do anything and sometimes restrains his power for reasons we rarely understand. In our confusion, we pray the embarrassing prayer of unsteady faith. It acknowledges our deficiency and asks for Christ to tend to it. It's a prayer he mercifully answers. "Help my unbelief."

Weak Faith in Our Strong God

It demonstrates a principle Pastor Jim Cymbala noted when he wrote, "I discovered an astonishing truth: God is attracted to weakness. He can't resist those who humbly and honestly admit how desperately they need Him."[3] The apostle Paul reiterated this truth as he wrestled with his own ongoing struggle with weakness. When he asked the Lord about it, God said, "My power is made perfect in weakness" (see 2 Corinthians 12:9). Brennan Manning paints the same picture when he writes, "Jesus comes not for the super-spiritual but for the wobbly and the weak-kneed who know they don't have it all together, and who are not too proud to accept the handout of amazing grace."[4]

What an amazing handout it is. It is the scandal by which we are saved through the faith God granted in the first place (see Ephesians 2:8). When we come to Jesus weak and wondering, whatever he accomplishes on our behalf is credited solely to him, for his glory and his fame. We are the grateful beneficiaries of his completed work. When we finally rest in knowing he is reliable and good, even as we struggle, we gain a willingness to receive mercy and grace, in any form he chooses. He gives an assurance of things hoped for, the conviction of things not yet seen (see Hebrews 11:1).

In a word, faith.

Faith that needs the help of a God who delights to give it.

Growing Faith

Refuse to be ashamed if you come to Jesus with questions and doubts, wondering if he can and if he will. It is not always for us to know the how, the why, or the when of his work. The fact that we seek him, with questions swirling about our hearts, is evidence of the seeds of faith planted and waking up in the fertile soil of trials and trouble.

He is the gardener who makes weak faith grow and calls his work remarkable.

—

Jesus,

Thank you for the circumstances of life that drive me to you. In desperation I ask you to rescue me from the terrors of sin and the scourge of unbelief. Disappointment, despair, and disease have sometimes pummeled my faith in you almost to death. I'm so thankful you are not put off by honesty. You desire truth in the inmost parts. Help me to be honest with myself so I can be honest with you.

Lord, I confess I have tried to manufacture faith and disguise my ignorance. You are not fooled. Please give me the courage to disclose my doubt and confess with stark honesty the true position of my heart. "I believe. Help my unbelief!"

Helpless Faith

The Paralyzed Man

A few days later, when Jesus again entered Capernaum, the people heard that he had come home. They gathered in such large numbers that there was no room left, not even outside the door, and he preached the word to them. Some men came, bringing to him a paralyzed man, carried by four of them. Since they could not get him to Jesus because of the crowd, they made an opening in the roof above Jesus by digging through it and then lowered the mat the man was lying on. When Jesus saw their faith, he said to the paralyzed man, "Son, your sins are forgiven."

Now some teachers of the law were sitting there, thinking to themselves, "Why does this fellow talk like that? He's blaspheming! Who can forgive sins but God alone?"

Immediately Jesus knew in his spirit that this was what they were thinking in their hearts, and he said to them, "Why are you thinking these things? Which is easier: to say to this paralyzed man, 'Your sins are forgiven,' or to say, 'Get up, take your mat and walk'? But I want you to know that the Son of Man has authority on earth to forgive sins." So he said to the man, "I tell you, get up, take your mat and go home." He got up, took his mat and walked out in full view of them all. This amazed everyone and they praised God, saying, "We have never seen anything like this!"

—Mark 2:1–12

Parallel passages: Matthew 9:1–8,

Luke 5:17–26

All day long he'd been aching for a distraction. Dear God, to think of something else, anything else. Now that he had it, he despised it. Hours of studying infinite cracks in the ceiling, the angle of the beams against the wall, the sunlight slowly sweeping across the wall in the shape of the window, it had all been interrupted by the buzzing of a fly. Then two.

He lay motionless watching the insects circle his toes, then dive out of sight. Though he couldn't feel them, he knew why they had come. Their intermittent buzzing, circling, and landing again was proof of bedsores on his heels. He was helpless to stomp the flies away. A third fly descended.

As soon as his brother came in from fishing, he would mention the sores. He concentrated on the outdoor sounds and listened for signals of his brother's return home.

If his brother could not come, he would send his nephew. If the fishing went long for both of them, sometimes his brother would send a cousin with a loaf of bread. Someone would come. They always did, and yet, he wondered if they secretly argued at the dock about whose turn it was, or who had the time.

I'm hungry. They fed him. *I'm thirsty.* They gave him a drink. *I have bedsores again.* They washed his feet and changed the blankets. It was a dirty and degrading task, and all he had to offer them was more need. Still, every day one of them came.

His helplessness was compounded by a heavy pressure on his chest. It stifled his breathing and compressed his heart. In his silent days at home he could hear his own heartbeat. It was rhythmic and consistent, but he couldn't deny that some pressure was bearing down. Though he could feel no pain, it still hurt to breathe. Undistracted by most other sensations, this one remained.

With backward glances, physicians, religious leaders, and even family had whispered the same accusation: "He'll never recover his health until he's forgiven." He'd had plenty of time on his mat to consider their words. Inhaling with great effort, he suspected it was the weight of a lifetime of sin bearing down on him. Paralysis was the proof—an unrelenting bodily reminder of his sick soul. If they were right, he was paralyzed by sin with no way to be rid of it.

He knew the truth about himself. He lied to his family about feeling pain just to gain their attention. He lied to them about feeling fine just to make them go away. He asked to be laid near the window to get some fresh air when he really wanted to feast his eyes on the young women walking toward the well. Wild jealousy flared when he saw his kind brother doing everything he could not.

Most days he justified these simple sins. He wasn't hurting anyone. On the holiest days of the year, when his family traveled to Jerusalem for Passover, or when they celebrated religious feasts at home, his guilt and shame worried him. That intangible pressure on his chest weighed heavier.

Several years earlier he'd asked his brother, nephew, and cousins to carry him to the temple in Jerusalem. Perhaps he could find forgiveness or healing there.

It was a three-day journey from Capernaum, and it was a jouncing and nauseating ride. A most miserable effort to receive forgiveness, he'd thought. Even after the long trip and the detailed sacrificial ritual, the pressure in his chest remained. *Am I forgiven?* He didn't know. One thing he knew for sure, when he left the temple his mat was still beneath him. He never asked to go along again.

Over time, hope for healing and forgiveness had been smothered into the dirt below his mat, and he lay there like a living gravestone, marking the death of hope.

Someday he would die and join hope in its grave. He'd thought to hurry that day by refusing food and water. It was no use. His brother would not stand for it, and he had no means to protest. So he continued to eat and drink whenever he was fed.

Hurried footsteps outside the door drew his attention away from the pressure and buzzing flies, but no one entered. For the past several days there had been so many people in the street. He wondered if the fishing had picked up again, but his brother kept reporting an average catch. Shouts in the street worried him, and he feared violence had broken out. Was something going wrong? Surely the Roman patrol would quell the ruckus, but he hadn't heard soldiers demanding order, nor the commotion of horses galloping through.

A murmuring group of men grew louder and closer. Finally, the latch was lifted, the door swung open, and the flies scattered. His brother entered, followed by his nephew and both cousins. Now he was certain something was wrong. They never came all at once.

"What is it?" He searched each face for a hint. His view from the floor revealed bearded chins. His nephew's smooth face, however, shone with anticipation, and bore the strain of a suppressed smile. It eased his mind and doubled his curiosity.

"What's wrong?" he asked again. His brother noticed

the flies and instructed his nephew to mix the salt scrub.

His brother knelt and unrolled a broiled fish. "Eat," his brother said and fed him a bite. Knowing there was no point refusing before getting an answer, he ate.

"Have you heard about a rabbi named Jesus of Nazareth?" his brother asked.

"I've heard the name." He swallowed the fish and asked, "Is he in the synagogue?"

"Sometimes." His brother paused, reached for the water jar, and dipped a drinking cup. "He's teaching and doing things we have never seen or heard." Cradling his helpless brother's shoulders, he held the cup to his lips, let him drink, laid him back down, and continued. "In the market, at the shore, in the synagogue, everyone is talking about him."

"Why?" He searched their faces for some clue.

"Because he is the one Moses and the prophets wrote about."

He showed no signs of teasing. How long had it been since Israel had heard from a prophet? Miraculous prophets were the subjects of stories handed down to children.

"Is he a fine teacher then?" he asked.

"Yes, but he's more." He wiped the paralyzed man's mouth. "He's healed many sick people."

"So he's a rabbi and a physician?"

"Yes, but…" He paused. "They say he is the Son of God."

The menacing pressure on his chest intensified. The Son of God? He raised his head to see if something heavy had been laid on him. It was only the weight of his clothes. Despite the suffocating pressure, his heart beat strong in his ears.

"The Son of God…," he repeated. He allowed himself one moment to imagine it. "I need to see him."

"I hoped you'd say that." His brother smiled. "We'll have to go today though. They say he leaves in the evenings and sometimes can't be found in the morning until word comes back that he's already crossed the lake or left the region. I'd rather carry you the length of Capernaum than have to take you down to Jerusalem again."

It was the first time his brother had ever mentioned the difficulty of that trip, and for the first time he realized it had not been easy for any of them.

"Then take me today."

Without a discussion, they each nodded.

His nephew finished with the salt, rinsed the sores, and situated a clean rolled cloth under his ankles to keep his heels off the mat. They dressed him in his other cloak and laid a fresh wool blanket on his mat.

"Ready?"

He nodded.

Each of them lifted an end of the two wooden poles that held his mat taut, then carried him out the door.

The afternoon sun was high and blinding. He shut his eyes as they maneuvered him down the street, trotting through Capernaum, dodging travelers and curious residents with every step. The paralyzed man blinked away the sunlight and dust as he bounced involuntarily with each advancing move. Muffled conversation swirled around him along with a fresh cloud of dust kicked up by the shuffling crowd. The dust choked him and forced a wheezing cough, drawing brief and disgusted stares. He closed his eyes again and listened.

His brother was right. Everyone was talking about Jesus of Nazareth. Some told secondhand stories of a leper who'd been made well, "leaping through the street on his way to the temple." "A woman suffering with fever immediately got up when he healed her!"

The stories surfaced like air bubbles from the bottom of a well—unexpected, unexplainable, provoking the curious to discover the source.

Skepticism was also in the air. Religious leaders from the surrounding area were also on their way. "If he were the Messiah, he would be in Jerusalem! These outlying cities are not fitting." The frame of his stretcher brushed them as they passed, and they glared. Facing rearward as they traveled, he had the disadvantage of seeing every contorted reaction as they passed. "At the very least, he ought to be in the synagogue," he heard another religious leader say.

It was true. Jesus was not in the synagogue. Word of his location had cut through the region, and people from every corner of Israel were running toward the neighbor's home where they finally located him.

The street in front of the house was churning with activity as people flooded the area. The magnitude of the crowd was frightening. A little girl tugged on her mother's cloak and demanded to be held. He wondered at the large crowd and the reason they hovered there. All the commotion he'd heard in the streets had been headed to this house, to see Jesus.

The thought bolstered his hope. If Jesus could heal,

then nothing was impossible for him. The thought startled him. Hope of recovery was long dead, or so he'd thought.

Pushing past those in the street, the four relatives navigated their passenger partway through the courtyard toward the front door. Instead of finding Jesus, they found the house overflowing. The crowd inside was backed up through the doorway, and the crowd outside pressed toward the house.

A few uncomfortable stragglers crammed themselves between the stone supports of the doorway sealing part of the crowd in and everyone else out. With no offer of sympathy, they looked down at the paralyzed man, then turned back toward the voice of the teacher inside. Disappointed but determined, the four maneuvered their passenger through the milling crowd to look for another entrance. Through a window they caught a glimpse of Jesus. "There he is!" his brother whispered.

"Where?" the helpless man asked, thinking maybe Jesus had come out of the house. He was teaching from the main room, surrounded by religious leaders dressed in garb that pronounced them as such, his brother explained. No doubt they'd gained easy access. Folks moved aside easily for them. Rounding the house they found no other entrance, only a growing crowd. They set the stretcher at the bottom of the stairs leading to the flat roof and rested.

Sitting on the step above him was his nephew. His chin rested in his cupped hand and from the ground, his face was mostly hidden. His tapping sandal revealed his troubled thoughts. "We can't leave," he petitioned his father.

"No," his father agreed, "but if we wait until the crowd has gone, Jesus may leave too."

His nephew eyed two pigeons bobbing and turning along the roofline. They scurried sideways along the edge and then flew away. He dropped his hand from his chin and looked at his father. "Could we go on the roof?" The others looked up, skeptical and humored. Defending his idea, he spoke again. "Well, we can't get in the door. We could dig through the thatching, lift the roof tiles, and ease him down."

Lying motionless, the paralyzed man swallowed a lump in his throat. He was touched by the young man's suggestion. His youth was naive and admirable. To dig an opening the size of a man was to damage the roof. He imagined them shuffling around on the roof causing mud and dust to rain on Jesus and those religious leaders around him. They wouldn't tolerate it. There was also the issue of getting him safely to the floor. He shook his head. The options weren't favorable, but something inside him couldn't dismiss the idea.

His brother knelt down to discuss it. Tension and concern were tangled in the wrinkles of his brow. Before his brother said a word, the paralyzed man consented by chiding, "Are you too weak to lift this skeleton?"

They devised their plan. The paralyzed man lay there unable to make any contribution apart from his consent. Humbled and saddened by the thought of it, he longed to hide his face, but he could not manage even that. He watched as each man removed his corded belt and secured it to the corners of his stretcher. Awkwardly and quietly they made their way up the stairs, despite scowls from suspicious bystanders.

Whispering about the exact location of Jesus in the house, they knelt to unearth the tiles and make an opening as long as a man.

He heard a dirt clod come loose from the ceiling and burst into pieces on the floor inside. A cool draft from inside the house drifted over him. Then with every ounce of strength and coordination, the four men lowered him through the hole in the roof.

The beams of the ceiling came into view, then the heads of those standing, then the faces of those seated, and finally, settling him on the floor, the men laid their silent request before Jesus.

Sunlight poured into the house and four silhouettes peeked through the broad opening and into the room below. He squinted as dust and debris from the dismantled roof swirled about the room.

When his eyes adjusted, he saw Jesus. He felt his chin quivering. Shame and regret mingled with incessant hopefulness as he lay before the Son of God.

His heart beat loudly, and sweat beaded upon his forehead and rolled toward his ears. Jesus showed no sign of agitation at the extraordinary interruption. Instead, he squinted through the sunlight now streaming through the gaping hole in the roof and smiled at the four relatives peering down upon the scene.

Jesus knelt beside the stretcher and placed his weathered hand on the paralytic's limp shoulder. Dispelling all the man's regret and fear, Jesus looked him in the eye and said, "Take courage, my son. Don't be afraid. Your sins are forgiven." He'd mentioned his sins to no one, yet Jesus knew. The heavy pressure lifted. Healing forgiveness washed over him like waves of fresh, clean air. It no longer hurt to breathe. He inhaled with ease. He'd done nothing to deserve it—hadn't traveled to the temple, hadn't brought a sacrifice. Even though his mat was still beneath him, he knew his sins had been dismissed.

He relished the relief, until he noticed the shifting religious leaders on the other side of him. Appalled at his interruption and his appearance, they backed away. One covered his mouth as if he were about to gag. He looked down at his own skin-covered skeleton, then at the stout legs and thick waists of those sitting on the floor and standing by. He was almost appalled at himself. He turned away from his shifting accusers, but he could not apologize for his spectacle. The weight was lifted.

He was forgiven.

Jesus also noticed their disapproval. Instead of averting his eyes, he looked at them directly. "Why are you reasoning like that and thinking evil in your hearts?" Jesus asked.

From his place on the floor, the paralyzed man could hardly bear their disgust. He watched them glance at each other, then at Jesus, and he realized they were not appalled at his floor-level spectacle. They were appalled at Jesus, the One who forgave his sin. Jesus challenged them, "Which is easier for me to say to him, 'Your sins are forgiven' or 'Get up and walk'?" They stewed in silence. Pride and confusion kept them from answering out loud, but the answer was painfully obvious. Absolutely anyone could merely speak the words, *Your sins are forgiven*. Jesus waited. Their only response was palpable indignation. He spoke again as if answering their silent questions. "I have the authority from God to forgive sin. And I will show you."

Turning back to the paralyzed man, Jesus said, "Get up," then he offered his hand. The paralyzed man found himself reaching for it. The sagging flesh on his arm appeared taut with muscle. He grasped Jesus' hand, gathered his legs beneath him, and stood. He towered above the religious leaders seated there. It was a view he'd never seen, a balding head, the seams of their religious headdresses. His entire scope of vision turned around by Jesus.

A collective gasp rose from the crowd. From above him, a joyful sob fell through the hole in the ceiling.

He stood eye to eye with Jesus. He wanted to shout

and whisper thanks, to jump with joy and kneel to honor. He was the first one worshipping through tears and a smile, completely mobile but paralyzed to know what to do first. Jesus saw his dilemma. "Pick up your stretcher and go home."

Four silhouettes disappeared from the hole in the roof and scuffled off the roof. The entire crowd was astounded. The folks inside, those crammed in the door and peeking through the window gasped and murmured, questioned and stared. Through astonished bits of laughter they declared to one another, "This is remarkable! We've never seen anything like this!"

He stooped to roll the wooden poles of his mat as though closing a scroll. Balancing them over his shoulder he walked toward the door. This time the crowd willingly made way for him.

He was forgiven, and Jesus had given more. He'd healed his body to prove he had the power to forgive his soul.

His brother, nephew, and cousins met him at the end of a long aisle of astonished witnesses. They wept, and hugged, and on their way home they pointed every traveler toward the house where Jesus was.

Two Kinds of Trouble

Daily he grappled with *why?* He spent hours consoling himself with dark thoughts of death and battled with sinful ideas, though he was unable to commit the sinful action. His mental agony was compounded by the spiritual anguish and the prevailing belief that physical sickness was always punishment for personal sin—a belief that God himself had refuted thousands of years earlier (see Job 42:7). Still it lingered as God's people clung to external indicators as proof of his approval or punishment.

This man was helpless to accomplish anything that other folks could applaud as service to God. He had no temple attendance, no kneeling in prayer, no money for an offering, no external evidence of righteousness, so they defaulted to what they could see—the outward evidence of what they believed was God's judgment.

While he was not privy to all that was whispered about him outside his four walls, he was intimately acquainted with every inconsolable thought clawing at the walls of his mind.

He had two impossible needs. One was physical, external, observable. His other need was spiritual, internal, unseen. He couldn't take too many Sabbath steps, couldn't commit adultery, and couldn't steal. Who knows a man's thoughts except the Spirit? The paralyzed man knew, and his soul sickness gnawed at his heart.

Holy Insensitivity

The surprising starting point of faith is to acknowledge inability, and to believe Jesus can do something about it. Their firm persuasion, based on a secondhand account, made these five men eager to see Jesus. So eager that when the Son of God came home to a neighbor's house, they made their request with a holy insensitivity. Through impatient shouldering, impolite interruptions, and deconstructing a structure, they laid their silent request before Jesus. One request was obvious and seen by all. The other request was seen only by Jesus and the man suffering under the weight of his unseen sin.

This was an encounter with the Great Physician, who addressed the most urgent need first. Like a case of internal bleeding or an obstructed airway, the symptoms of soul sickness were not immediately obvious to the untrained eye, and if not treated the results would be fatal.

The holy eyes of the Great Physician diagnosed it before anyone could describe symptoms. He saw a heart obstructed by sin, and a man frightened by it. Jesus could also see invisible faith. As was his life's purpose, he healed the most damning disease first, and saved this man from his sins. "Don't be afraid, Friend. Your sins are forgiven" (Matthew 9:2, AMP).[5] Everyone crowded in that room was either disappointed or incensed. Everyone except for the forgiven man.

Though Christ is never bound to our wishes, for this man, he went beyond forgiveness. Jesus didn't intend to entertain the crowd with a miracle. He wasn't repaying the paralytic for worthy service. Jesus wasn't even responding to a verbal request. Jesus healed the man to declare to skeptical observers that he was God. He came to save his people from their sins, and the paralyzed man became the blessed object lesson.

If the incensed religious leaders hadn't been so determined to save themselves by rituals and rules, they would have seen Jesus came to save them too, if only they would admit their inability to save themselves. The paralyzed man had the advantage of knowing true helplessness.

Invisible Injury

We sometimes believe our most urgent trouble is a circumstance, a relationship, or an obvious injury. Oftentimes these are the conditions that bring us to Jesus' divine procedure room.

We want him to alleviate the pain of all our heavy circumstances, but he sees we need to be relieved of the slavish drive to deserve something he insists is a free gift. We think we need to work harder to prove ourselves, but he sees we need to rest in the fact that he is doing the work. The Great Physician sees the invisible injury, and so he allows the outward illness to show us the inward one. Then he tends to our healing with grace and mercy.

When we lay ourselves in his way, we proclaim to the world that we are dependent, and that he is strong and reliable. In doing so, we glorify him. Instead of being an interruption or hindrance, we become the grateful recipients of forgiveness, healing, whatever treatment he renders. As we follow the orders of our generous Caregiver, we are able to walk away from sin, freed from slavish duty, and delighted to share him with all who need his care.

Remarkable Acts of Faith

Helpless faith hasn't accomplished remarkable "acts of faith," but helpless faith also realizes that "acts of faith" are not prerequisites to forgiveness. We recognize we haven't done anything to earn God's favor. We can't do anything to earn his favor, but we come to him anyway, asking to receive forgiveness, healing, and help because he delights to give it. In the silence of our own hearts, without even the work of words, we are helpless to earn his forgiveness, yet happy to receive it. That is the essence of remarkable faith.

~

Lord,

Like the paralytic, I often wallow in regret and wish the situation were different. Sometimes my crippling circumstances are a result of my love for sin. Other times they are the repercussions of living in a world poisoned by it.

Thank you for the gift of those who care for my soul and lead me to you. Thank you for those who urge me to believe in my heart what my eyes have not yet seen.

Thank you for seeing invisible faith. Strengthen my faith so that I may stand in awe of your remarkable forgiveness and point others to you.

Unworthy Faith

The Roman Centurion

When Jesus had finished saying all this to the people who were listening, he entered Capernaum. There a centurion's servant, whom his master valued highly, was sick and about to die. The centurion heard of Jesus and sent some elders of the Jews to him, asking him to come and heal his servant. When they came to Jesus, they pleaded earnestly with him, "This man deserves to have you do this, because he loves our nation and has built our synagogue." So Jesus went with them.

He was not far from the house when the centurion sent friends to say to him: "Lord, don't trouble yourself, for I do not deserve to have you come under my roof. That is why I did not even consider myself worthy to come to you. But say the word, and my servant will be healed. For I myself am a man under authority, with soldiers under me. I tell this one, 'Go,' and he goes; and that one, 'Come,' and he comes. I say to my servant, 'Do this,' and he does it."

When Jesus heard this, he was amazed at him, and turning to the crowd following him, he said, "I tell you, I have not found such great faith even in Israel." Then the men who had been sent returned to the house and found the servant well.

—Luke 7:1–10

Parallel Passage: Matthew 8:5–13

As the sun disappeared below the western horizon, the centurion removed his flashing bronze helmet with its yellow crest of horsehair still standing at attention and stepped inside the door of his house. He raked fingers through his sweaty hair. With half his men deployed throughout the town for the night, his duties were fulfilled until sunrise, barring any skirmishes.

A servant hurried to his side to help remove his armor.

"How is he?" the centurion asked the servant.

"Not good. It may be tonight."

"Well…keep him hydrated." It was a weak order, he knew, but they looked to him for direction. He shook his head, refusing defeat. Shedding the rest of his armor, he went to his library.

He rolled out a map of the city to review the day's work. The bold Roman script across the top proclaimed his home away from Rome: Capernaum. It was not the adventure of the Frontiers of the Empire, but also none of the discomforts. Bloodshed was minimal in Capernaum, so his duties and those of his one hundred soldiers were mainly to keep order. On top of the map he rolled open his daily record of disputes, arrests, and skirmishes and made notes about how each was resolved by his men.

Unwilling taxpayer near the lake detained. Taxes successfully extracted.

Unruly drunkard defiling synagogue. Arrested and jailed.

Pottery crashed in the hall, and a scream jerked him from his records. Instinctively he drew his dagger, then put it back in its sheath. It was not an intruder. The flurry of scuffling feet in the next room confirmed it. He went to ensure order was restored. His servant girls scurried around the room like beetles scrambling under a lifted rock, tossing shards of the broken jar into its jagged base, fetching water, dipping rags, and swabbing the forehead of his sick and thrashing servant.

The man was paralyzed yet not without movement. He shivered with fever and cried out. Without warning he jerked involuntarily. Sickness mounted a violent coup against his body, and nothing was able to quell the brutality. The servants struggled to restrain his movement and keep him still. They maneuvered him into proper position on the bed while he made unintelligible complaints. Then, overcome by pain, he passed out limp. They worked to lay him straight, repositioned his arms, and untangled the blankets while he was still.

Even to a soldier hardened by war and peacekeeping, it was unbearable to watch. This was not his enemy or a zealous rebel to be controlled.

This was his most trusted servant. A strong, honest, and responsible man who'd never given him a reason to question. In family matters he maintained every confidence. In finances he was a wise steward. In civilian and political affairs he was an insightful advisor. He maintained all authority in the centurion's absence and had garnered respect and trust from his fellow household servants as well as the centurion's own family. He displayed qualities that could not be taught or trained. He was irreplaceable. Though he'd never utter the words aloud, he considered him a confidant and, more importantly, a friend. He'd spared no expense for doctors and medications, all to no avail. Water, cool rags, and attentive care were all he had left to offer.

When the guest room settled, he returned to his table covered with maps and searched for a distraction. His patrol records would do. He continued where he'd left off and found more entries than usual. Besides the familiar complaints of Roman oppression and taxes, crowds converged in nearly every locale—on the shore, near the mountains, in the city, and in homes. At the center was a Jewish teacher named Jesus. He went by several titles: Son of David, Jesus of Nazareth, and some plainly called him rabbi—teacher.

Reports about his authoritative teaching had ripped through the city, drawing masses from surrounding districts. They clamored to absorb his every word. Parading every sort of infirmity before him, they begged for healing. Though it always caused a civil disturbance, the crowds that formed around Jesus were not angry mobs that irked the Roman government. The curious crowds included the young, old, sick, healthy, rich, and poor.

The Jewish people had endeared themselves to the centurion. They were a careful and moral lot. Strict adherence to their strange customs gave a sense of civil order—a top priority to the ruling Romans. Truthfully, they made his duties easier. To show his appreciation and encourage their worship, he'd financed the construction of their synagogue. In its planning stages, he'd learned much about these people and their One and Only God. They told of ancient wartime victories their God had granted. A young shepherd with a rod and sling defeated a giant Philistine warrior. Ancient Jericho fell when they marched around the city according to their God's unusual orders. The wildest tale was their escape from the Egyptians when their God dried up the sea and they marched through the middle on dry land. They revered their God. Even in the construction of the synagogue, they never uttered their God's name aloud and upheld his law with meticulous care. As a Roman—Gentile, as they called him—he was never actually allowed in the synagogue after it was completed. Only Jews were allowed inside. On a calm day, though, the teaching could be heard outdoors.

He kept careful watch on the building and the worshippers. The last time they'd patrolled the narrow streets surrounding the synagogue he'd heard Jesus called by another name. It had been the Jewish Sabbath, a day that was usually quiet. As he and his men rounded the corner a shriek—or possibly a howl—rolled out of the synagogue into the streets with the words, "What do you want with us, Jesus of Nazareth?" The guttural shrieking continued. "I know who you are—the Holy One of God!"

Since Jewish law forbade them to enter, out of respect, he didn't immediately command an investigation. But they had stopped in the street, at the ready, if any violence broke out. None did. He held his men in formation outside, partly out of duty, partly out of curiosity. The mystery of what had happened inside the synagogue was revealed by fragmented conversation as the crowd filed out. "At his word!…And with such authority!…He commands the evil spirits and they come out!"

So that's what they'd heard. The shriek of a demon. Though the centurion had seen evil upon evil, it still made him shudder. According to the reports billowing into the street, Jesus faced his enemy with power and authority. Jesus, the Holy One of God, had not shuddered. With a word, not a weapon, he commanded a demon, and by all accounts it had followed orders. A tormented soul was rescued and restored.

The centurion dropped the patrol record and glanced toward the guest room. He'd found a strategy.

Before the sun had fully risen the next morning, he sent for several prominent Jewish leaders he'd met during the synagogue construction. With their social and religious standing, they would have no trouble gaining an audience with Jesus. Since Jewish law and their traditions barred him from the synagogue, how much more unworthy was he to approach their powerful teacher himself? He determined not to offend the only one who could help.

When the Jewish elders arrived at his house, he dispensed with pleasantries and explained the gravity of his servant's condition. "There isn't much time left for him, I'm afraid. Would you go for me and ask this authoritative teacher to come and heal my servant? Today."

He could tell the Jewish elders were glad their help was necessary. Their involvement gave them leverage. He'd seen the same patronizing smile on the face of his commander when he was in training. He'd seen it again on the battlefield on the face of an informant. It was the feigned worry of the opportunist. He knew the favor would cost him. Maybe he would waive a tax or repair the synagogue. In any case, he needed their cooperation. No respectable Jewish teacher would enter the house of a non-Jew—an officer of the Roman Empire, no less.

"Perhaps we can convince him to come." They hurried off to locate the milling crowd who always betrayed Jesus' whereabouts.

The centurion watched them go and dared to hope he would soon receive word. Jesus commanded authority. He was powerful. But more powerful than that? In the guest room, no one was stirring as they had been the night before. Holding his breath for a moment, he waited, and then saw his trusted servant's chest rise with the smallest breath. He was uncomfortable eavesdropping on the suffering, and at the same time comforted. It was not too late. He strode to the front gate and saw his messengers disappear down the street and around the corner. They were on their way.

He paced from his table full of maps, past the damp air of the guest room, back to the front gate for a look. Nothing. Perhaps Jesus would refuse. Jews hated the Romans and he was undeniably Roman. He knew the exploits of his own cohort were deplorable to them. He'd been the purveyor of the atrocities of war and occupation. All the blood, death, and decay—everything the Jews were so careful to avoid—he had wallowed in it. Sending the Jewish elders had been his best choice. Hadn't it?

He reconsidered his options. Perhaps it was bad strategy not sending some offer for Jesus. What could he offer a man with such authority? Money? Bribery wouldn't convince one undaunted by devils. His pondering brought him back to his first position. He felt no better than a beggar. The feeling was strange and unfamiliar.

The approaching footsteps sounded like a hundred undisciplined soldiers, and when he marched back to the door he saw the crowd, happy and curious, clamoring for the attention of the man being ushered toward his house. One of the Jewish elders hurried ahead of the crowd and met the centurion at his gate. "He has agreed to come heal your servant!"

While the household servants gushed over the Jewish elder and the good news, the centurion spoke not with gratitude, but with cautious surprise.

"How did you convince him?"

"We explained your love for our people and that you built our synagogue. I said to him myself, 'If any foreigner is worthy of your time, Jesus, surely it's this centurion!' "

He slammed the gate, and turned toward the house. What had he done? The Holy One entrusted with power from God was on his way, thinking a Roman centurion was worthy of his time. "No. No. Nothing could be further from the truth. I am not worthy. You elders ought to know that!" Shaking his head, the centurion stifled frustration and drew in his breath.

Two trusted friends had come prepared to mourn the dying servant. They sat in the courtyard awaiting his call. He had different orders for them now.

"Friends!" He summoned them.

He stared at the baffled Jewish elder, making sure he was listening, but spoke to his friends.

"Hurry to deliver this message to Jesus with the utmost care toward its content and with reverent respect to its recipient. Repeat these exact words as my representatives: 'Sir, contrary to what you have been told, I am not worthy to have you come under my roof. This is precisely why I did not presume to approach you myself. Still, I beg for your help. I know that if you simply say the word you can heal my servant. I know this because, like you, I am a man under authority, and I have soldiers in my charge as well. I say to one, "go" and he goes; and to another "come" and he comes. I say to this servant "do this," and he does it. I know that you are the Holy One of God and have authority to command devils or healing even from a distance. Please, do not trouble yourself to come to my house.' Now go."

Then, as if dressing his words in flesh, they went.

He retreated to the house and stationed himself at the front window. He watched his friends approach the crowd. When they met the entourage led by Jesus, he heard them deliver the message. Verbatim. The two Jewish elders on either side of Jesus squirmed with irritation at the blatant contradiction to the account they'd just put forth.

Jesus gave a perceptive nod to the centurion's friends. With astonishment in his tone he faced those following him—his disciples, a band of formerly disabled, and pious citizens.

The centurion hushed his breathing and strained to hear him over the shifting of the crowd halted in the street. They had come the distance from the corner but had not reached his courtyard. He saw Jesus smile, shake his head, then pause for a moment before he spoke.

Had he offended Jesus? He'd been so careful not to.

"Astonishing!" he heard Jesus say. "Not even in Israel, among my own people, not even among any of you, have I found such great faith!" He spoke to the centurion's friends and pointed toward the house. "Go. Tell the centurion I will do what he believed I could do."

They rushed back to the house. The centurion met his friends at the gate, but before he could discuss what had transpired, he heard an urgent call.

"Sir!" It was a servant girl. "Come quickly."

They all rushed inside. Her face was pale as she directed them to the guest room where, on the guest bed, sat his most trusted servant—his friend—taking a long draw on a pitcher of water. He wiped his face with his sleeve and thanked the servant girl. When he noticed the centurion looking in, he got up from the bed. He smiled and said, "I guess I've been out of commission for a while."

The centurion was weak with relief. "Yes, you have."

Evidence of Jesus' healing authority stood before him. He felt a delightful shortness of breath and heavy hush in his soul. The Holy One of God commanded authority, the likes of which the centurion was not worthy to host. Jesus gave orders to sickness and disease and they obeyed him—even from a distance.

The centurion knelt to honor the authority he would gladly serve.

You Get What You Deserve (or Do You?)

With only a shallow knowledge of the true God, this centurion understood his own position before God better than the religious leaders who claimed to be God's privileged people. The religious elders were governed by this assumption: God would do what they wanted if they did what God wanted. It was a transaction. By their outward behaviors and religious checklists—the pretense that they were serving God—they presumed they could manipulate God. Jesus did not act as they expected, so they determined he was not from God, and certainly wasn't the expected Messiah.

They grew even more furious when Jesus said the religious leaders did everything for people to see, from the clothes they wore, to the prayers they prayed, to the places they sat (see Matthew 23:5–7). It was all to impress. They displayed good external religion to earn praise from the people they ruled and to earn the favor of God—in short, to serve their own interests.

The centurion, on the other hand, understood that authority was given for service. The authority given to the centurion by Rome was meant to serve the interests of the empire, not the personal interests of the centurion. Centurions served the empire, not the other way around. He understood what it meant to be under authority, to take orders and carry them out without question. Rebellion meant dismissal and probably death. Rome could not be manipulated. But Rome was also powerless to save his servant, so the centurion appealed to someone more powerful than Rome. One who commanded authority on earth and received his authority from heaven.

No currency, no transaction, would put Jesus in his service, and he knew it. No one could do or repay what he was asking of Jesus, so he appealed to Jesus with nothing to offer in return.

And Jesus marveled. That Jesus would marvel at anything he saw on earth should give us pause. He had enjoyed the glories of heaven. What on earth would he have marveled about?

The centurion recognized Jesus' power to work miracles, but that recognition was not unique. Jesus had seen that the crowds who followed him all over Israel also recognized his miracle-working power. Jesus did not marvel at the folks who followed him for the entertainment. He called them wicked and adulterous (see Matthew 12:39). The centurion had built a synagogue and loved the Jewish nation. The influential religious leaders were impressed, but Jesus didn't marvel at the centurion's generosity and goodwill.

What caused Jesus to marvel was "such great faith." It was the centurion's genuine deference and clear understanding that Christ was entrusted with power from God. Such faith was uncommon in Israel. If it was there, Jesus said he hadn't seen it yet. But here—outside Jerusalem, outside the temple and the synagogue, outside their religious community—was a man who recognized who he was in comparison to Jesus. He did not compare himself to the religious leaders. He compared himself with Christ. In doing so, he saw great similarity and shocking contrast.

The centurion had been entrusted with the authority of Rome.

Christ had been entrusted with the authority of God.

The centurion commanded soldiers.

Christ commands disease, demons, and death.

The centurion was an ambassador of Roman glory.

Christ was the exact representation of God's glory (see Hebrews 1:3).

His careful assessment gave him an accurate view of himself. He knew he was undeserving, and instead of despairing, he appealed to Christ anyway. "His combination of humility, dependent request, and trusting awareness of God's power is the essence of faith."[6]

In Christ, You Don't Get What You Deserve

As twenty-first-century believers we are often tossed around by messages presented to us from every direction about our worth. Some advertisers have us believe we are worth little without their product. Others try to convince us that we are so worthy we deserve their services.

We must look to our Chief Commander to find out what is true. We must not compare ourselves to others—Christians or non-Christians. We must make an assessment of ourselves in comparison to Christ. Only then will we discover the truth that we actually deserve spiritual death (see Romans 6:23). It's what we've earned. But God is merciful, and Jesus was obedient to his orders. He came to rescue us from what we'd earned and deserved. He generously offers what we do not deserve and cannot earn: grace.

Grace by definition is an undeserved gift. "The moment we have to do something to make ourselves more acceptable to God, or the moment we have to have a certain feeling or attribute of character in order to be blessed by God, then grace is no longer grace."[7] Then "grace" becomes something we believe we deserve. It becomes something we have earned that God is obligated to pay. This was the error of the religious leaders, and an ongoing, though subtle, error we find even in our own hearts some two thousand years later.

Who Instills Worth?

Whether you've built a synagogue, an orphanage, or a fine Christian reputation, you cannot earn God's favor. God's grace to us in Christ is a gift! We are worthy because we acknowledge our continual need of Jesus Christ and because he has declared us worthy! It is only by his declaration that we can come boldly to God. Though we are undeserving, we are privileged to belong to God and worthy because of Jesus.

The Gift You Cannot Earn

We cannot place God in our service by stockpiling good deeds and dangling them before him as a currency, as though we hold the carrot that makes him do our bidding. Our "good deeds" are not a means to get what we want from God. He has completely nullified that strategy by his grace through Jesus Christ.

He asks us to come to him without pointing to accomplishments or reasons that supposedly make us "deserving." We must come with an accurate understanding of his authority over us. We don't deserve his grace, but he continues to lavish it on his dependent children.

———

Oh Lord,

Your power and authority are beyond words or comprehension.

With the centurion I confess I am an unworthy host. Your holiness exposes my sinfulness, and I am not worthy to approach you. I have nothing to offer that would merit your favor. Nothing I do can make me worthy of you.

But by the cross you declare me worthy. You made me holy. You offer to live with me, in me. Instead of offering you a gift, I receive your gift of grace.

Help me submit to the wild ways of your power and authority. Help me to trust, like the centurion, that neither time nor distance, neither race nor creed, can limit the scope of your rule.

Help me follow his marvelous example of faith.

Suffering Faith

The Hemorrhaging Woman

A large crowd followed and pressed around him. And a woman was there who had been subject to bleeding for twelve years. She had suffered a great deal under the care of many doctors and had spent all she had, yet instead of getting better she grew worse. When she heard about Jesus, she came up behind him in the crowd and touched his cloak, because she thought, "If I just touch his clothes, I will be healed." Immediately her bleeding stopped and she felt in her body that she was freed from her suffering.

At once Jesus realized that power had gone out from him. He turned around in the crowd and asked, "Who touched my clothes?"

"You see the people crowding against you," his disciples answered, "and yet you can ask, 'Who touched me?'"

But Jesus kept looking around to see who had done it. Then the woman, knowing what had happened to her, came and fell at his feet and, trembling with fear, told him the whole truth. He said to her, "Daughter, your faith has healed you. Go in peace and be freed from your suffering."

—Mark 5:21–34

Parallel Passages: Matthew 9:20–22,

Luke 8:40–56

She laid her palm on the cool wall to steady herself and catch her breath. She blinked away the darkness creeping in from the outside edges of her vision. *Breathe.* She drew in a long breath and released it slowly. Clear vision returned and she pushed open her door.

The ground-level room she rented opened directly into a well-traveled street. If she could walk past all the houses to her right, she would eventually find the market, where merchants sold fruit and almonds, fish and lamb, cloth and baskets. If she could walk far enough down the road to her left, she would be on the shore of the Sea of Galilee with a hundred fishermen hollering to each other. She couldn't see it from her doorway, but on a calm day when the street was empty, she could hear them barking at one another for riggings and nets, at the bow and in the stern, then cursing the wind when it ruined their plans.

Both the market and the shore were an easy walk for a person in good health, but the eight steps from her bed to the door made her light-headed. She stepped outside and closed the door behind her.

A large crate butted up against the outside wall of her house. In the bustling morning commotion, no one would notice if she just sat there. She had a clear view of the street leading to the shore of Galilee, so she could be sure not to miss anything. It was the perfect place to rest and wait. She sat down, already tired, just steps from her own doorway. She tightened her cloak around her shoulders. She was cold. Always cold. With her back against the shaded wall, she shivered more than usual.

Despite her chill, she inhaled the morning breeze rolling off the lake. Fresh fish. There must have been a large catch last night. The smell stirred childhood memories of her mother bartering with the fish vendor. She recalled standing on tiptoe, at just the right height to rest her chin on the table and peer into the red eyes of her scaly lunch. If she was hungry, their flapping tails didn't even frighten her.

Her stomach growled. It had been years since she'd been to the market where villagers bustled and vendors bargained. The thought of it wore her out anyway. She wasn't welcome there so she stayed away. Occasionally on the evening before the Sabbath, after sunset when the vendors were cloistered at home preparing to rest, if she felt strong enough she would make the short but arduous journey to the empty market. On her knees in the dust she'd comb through the dirt under their vacant tables. Sometimes she'd find a stale piece of bread, or a half-eaten fig left by a gorged mouse. A stray coin was more common, but she couldn't eat that. Unclean women were forbidden in the market, so she couldn't spend it either. With no mother, no father, no siblings, no husband or children, she couldn't even give it to someone for her errand. She was poor, isolated, and unclean because of her condition.

At first her condition was an embarrassment, an inconvenience. Her monthly flow seemed to last longer than other girls her age. Mother schooled her in caring for herself, physically and then religiously.

"You can worship at synagogue only after the bleeding has stopped for seven days. Then your time of impurity is over."

When she questioned her mother, the response was curt. "That is the Law. We can't defile what is holy. God requires purity."

She watched her family leave for worship without her.

When she was a little girl, her mother's days of impurity were an annoyance. Her mother could always nurse and hold the babies, but she couldn't sit on her mother's lap, lie in her mother's bed, or even wrap herself in her mother's cloak or she too would become unclean. If she did, she had to endure the tedious washing ritual that stole her playtime. Her mother's constant chiding echoed in her mind like an ominous chant. "Don't touch my cloak." "No hugs today." "I can't join you at synagogue until I'm clean."

After she'd entered womanhood herself, the chiding became more personal and accusatory. "Sit in the next room." "Take care you don't touch that." She no longer feared being infected with impurity. She was now the carrier, the infector, and she knew the consequences of touching anyone. This religious community had no room for questionable perceptions.

Once her bleeding had stopped for a day. With anticipation she counted the days that would mark her purity. It never came. The bleeding returned before the seven days were over. What was once a welcome sign of fertility and the prospect of marriage was now a lonely pathway to the grave. Unclean. Impure. Unfit for worship. The words rang in her ears as she waited on the crate.

In those first months she dutifully carried out her cleansing routine. She scrubbed and wrung her clothing. She hung the bedding out and folded when it was dry. *Perhaps next week there will not be so much washing.* She longed for her mother's arms, even her father's rough hands. But she was unclean.

As her bleeding increased, her energy waned. The wash piled up and new stains darkened old ones. With no prospects for her health, let alone marriage or children, her father spoke with her about leaving home. She'd agreed, thinking it would be easier to function in solitude. She had little energy left for concerning herself with others.

Her dowry, now useless, was awarded to her rather than a potential husband. She sold every piece of jewelry and linen that had been saved for her wedding.

With the money, she secured her small room on the busy street. The remainder was spent to finance her healing, and her location provided easy access to a long line of eager physicians. Some she sent for specifically. Some must have heard about her plight and found her by hearing from another. Every one of them claimed to have the cure, for a price. "A glass of wine with a whole onion daily," one declared. He recommended a pestle and mortar for crushing the onion and a special wine. She bought it all.

Her hopes were pinned on a mixture she could make herself. She chopped and mashed the onion. Wiping her watering eyes with the back of her wrist she dumped the mash into a bowl. She poured enough wine into the bowl to make it drinkable. Wine bled into the onion pulp, and she mixed it thoroughly and took a sip. "Ahhhgh." She gasped, and her eyes watered again. Dabbing her eyes with her sleeve, she drank a long, big swallow. The mixture was sour and strong, thick and pink. It was a chore, but not as difficult as continuing to bleed, she told herself. She forced her mind to take a lovely walk to the shore, while her body guzzled the task at hand. It was down, and she was nauseated. The concoction boiled in her stomach, and she vomited. The force of it only increased the bleeding, and after a few days she stopped the treatment when she became too weak to mix the drink.

Crushed flowers, powdered minerals, and a host of other unidentified treatments staved off the hunger, and held out the promise of health, but every effort cost her, and every effort failed. For twelve years she bled. All she had left was to beg the God of her childhood. The One who had dried up the sea to save his people and stopped up a river to show them a new life. So she prayed. "You stopped the flow of the Jordan River. You can stop my suffering!"

But he didn't.

Supposing she lacked what God required, she sequestered herself in her cell, where all four walls and everything inside them bore the stains and the stench of her impurity. Unclean. Impure. Unfit for worship.

A familiar cramp kneaded its way through her lower back and thighs as she waited outside her front door. She curled toward her knees and tightened her arms around her thin waist. *A little longer. He is coming.*

Yesterday, an old physician had stopped by with a bit of news from the outside. He'd come to "monitor your plight" as he put it. As he unpacked his herbs and bottles, she warned him she had no money left for treatment or advice. She almost pitied him as he scurried to repack. *Monitor my plight.* She glared from her bed. *Don't you mean monitor my purse?* She held her tongue. She was too tired to argue.

He tied his cloak and rambled. "Well, I'll be going then. There are so many sick, you know. The treatments are scant and expensive. Patients must have their treatment, and treatment is never free." He stopped his scurrying and waved a crooked finger at her. "You remember that." He fetched the sandals he'd just removed and continued his warning. "There is a hoax circulating. Just yesterday it was rumored that a chained lunatic from the caves of Gadara was healed by the rabbi they call Jesus of Nazareth. Ha! How can anything good come from Nazareth?" He tucked his money pouch into his belt. "And they say he required no payment!" He huffed. "Health without medicine or money. I'll believe it when I see it." He laughed. "Perhaps I shall." He stopped scrambling and reported, "They've chased him out of Gadara and now he flees to us. To work his free and devilish magic no doubt!" He hoisted his bag over his shoulder. "Son of David, indeed!" He shook his head as if to rid his mind of the pestilent thought and opened the door. "Do you expect to receive any money from your family soon?"

"No," she whispered.

"Oh my. Well, I don't know if I'll return then." The door slammed and blew a thick cloud of dust to settle in place of his nervous scuttle. Her room was quiet again.

Jesus went to Gadara?

He was peculiar. It wasn't the first strange thing she'd heard about this teacher called Jesus of Nazareth. He drew a large congregation whenever he taught at the synagogue in Capernaum. She'd heard folks in the street saying he could heal the sick. No one went to Gadara on purpose. Did they? It was a cauldron of madmen, disease, and death. She imagined an impoverished madman, healed, unchained, and free to leave his cavernous prison.

She'd slept fitfully last night as the old physician's ramblings collided with scriptures from her childhood. A Nazarene? Son of David? What good news for a poor madman! Both mind and heart had been bound up by Jesus. He was liberated from the dark prison of the Gadarene caves. The words of Isaiah jumped from her memory and startled her.

The Spirit of the Sovereign Lord is on me,
because the Lord has anointed me
to proclaim good news to the poor.
He has sent me to bind up the brokenhearted,
To proclaim freedom for the captives
And release from darkness for the prisoners,
To proclaim the year of the Lord's favor…
—Isaiah 61:1

Her heart thumped, and a healthy dose of nervous nausea tickled her stomach as she had lain down for the night. Was this the year? Could he be? The Messiah?

Those churning thoughts kept her awake too long last night. Now her head ached with fatigue. Although her frailty was obvious, her sickness was on the inside. If she was careful, it couldn't be seen. If she could rest and appear well, perhaps she could hide her bleeding long enough to blend into the crowd.

Would they notice? Would they know? If the Spirit

of the Lord was with Jesus, he would know. He would know her plight, her impurity, her audacity, and her sin. What then?

She was unclean. What if she were exposed? They would stone her for sure. They'd take her outside the city and hurl a mountain of stones to mark her grave. If she could get near Jesus, though, just near enough to reach him, he could save her from death— whether by stoning, starvation, or bleeding. She should not touch him, or anyone else in the crowd, but if he came, as the old physician said, she would not miss him.

The street had quieted as fish buyers hurried to the shore to examine the night's catch. A synagogue leader rushed past without noticing her. Whether he meant to welcome Jesus or be first in line, she didn't know. He did not seem skeptical of trickery like the old doctor had warned.

She rubbed her temples and rested her face in her hands. She would not draw attention to herself. *If I can just touch his clothes, I will get well.* Tilting her head back against the wall, she rested.

She woke with a start to the din of a swelling crowd returning from the shore. Then she saw him, preceded by a group of boys, flanked by men directing the crowd, and followed by a great sea of people. Prayer tassels hung from the corners of his robe sweeping the road as if to clear the way. It was him. The Messiah, disguised as an ordinary rabbi.

She estimated the crowd's dizzying pace and accounted for her fatigue. She would join the happy throng and reach out as he passed by. As she stood, blood rushed from her body. Surveying her outer garments, she gathered her cloak. It was still clean.

Five boys ran ahead, kicking rocks and laughing. It was her cue. She stepped into the street. Joining the crowd, she held her head high and mimicked their enthusiasm. *Don't be noticed*, she told herself. *Don't stand out.* The risk was great. Her clothes hung off of her like linens draped on a post. Brittle hair escaped her head scarf and threatened to expose her for what she was. Unclean. Impure. Unfit for worship.

She was tossed along and waded toward him. As she got closer to Jesus, the jostling crowd became more vigorous, and she was taken up into their current. Jesus was just steps away, and she had no strength to fight her way to him. Just when she feared she may lose sight of him, he slowed. A clumsy group of them failed to notice and thrust her forward. Weary reflexes failed, and she tumbled to the ground. Her palms and elbows skidded through the dirt and broke her fall. Sandals scuffled around her and tripped and skipped long enough to redirect their course.

"Clumsy woman," one said. The crowd paused around her for a moment and one by one began to step around.

She surveyed her skinned arms. She was bleeding from within and bleeding from without. It was too much. She swallowed a sob, wiped her eyes with bloodied hands, and looked for a way out. Gathering her last shred of strength, she prepared to stand, when movement near the ground caught her eye. Through blurring tears she noticed the dancing tassels of a rabbi's robe. Immediately she reached out and grabbed his dusty hem. No sooner had she grasped it than his next step jerked it from her hand.

She squeezed her eyes shut to keep out the dust. In the darkness, her ears rang with silence. She felt warm, flushed, and strong. The kneading pain in her back and thighs stopped. She scrambled out of the dirt, easily freeing herself from the tangle of limbs and robes. She stood and felt no blood flow.

She was well. It was him. She had the urge to shout,

squeal, and cry for joy. Instead she sealed her lips, covered her quivering mouth, and summoned all her new strength to hold it in. She withdrew from the crowd. With her first strong step toward home, she heard him ask, "Who touched me?"

The surging crowd stopped. She choked back a cry wondering whether she should run to escape with her health, or run to the One who healed.

Everyone denied it. So unaccustomed to touching, she almost denied it herself. Every man speaking may well have touched him as the crowd flowed down the street. Then one of the men asked him, "Master, what do you mean? You know everyone is pressing in on you like grapes in a winepress. What do you mean by asking who touched you? We've all touched you."

Because he knows! her mind was screaming.

Jesus searched the crowd and replied, "No. Someone did touch me. It was a different touch. I felt power go out of me."

He knew. She knew.

Bewildered mothers questioned their children. Grown men shrugged and waited, and Jesus continued scanning the crowd.

Her hands and legs shook, though not with the weakness of lost blood, but with the weakness of worship. She pushed back into the crowd and threw herself at his feet, this time on purpose. "It was me!" she sobbed. Even the tassels on his hem seemed to stop dancing at the admission. She clasped her hands to stop the shaking. She wanted to touch him again, to thank him, to worship. She could only cry.

The crowd hushed. Now seeing her stained cloak they backed away from both of them and waited for Jesus to respond. She was exposed.

Jesus knelt to hear the whole truth of her broken story. He took her hand and helped her stand. His warmth melted her. The first willing touch in twelve years. "My daughter," he said, "you are healed of your disease, and now you may go home in peace, because I have made you clean."

Then he turned to go. The crowd engulfed him again, and he was gone.

He had healed her—bound up her broken heart and body. With a blessing of peace, he released her from the condemning prison of her room and liberated her to worship. She was clean. She was pure, and she would always worship.

Suffering for Obedience

What a way to live. Isolated. Unclean. Untouchable. She suffered because she was following God's laws. Why? It is, as Philip Yancey says, "The question that never goes away." Why would God require the people he rescued to suffer under such a heavy burden as the Law? When God first gave the Law of Moses to his chosen people they viewed him with frightening reverence. His terrifying power demanded it.

The Israelites overheard the collective wailing as one Egyptian mother after another found her oldest son lying in his bed, dead. They gawked as the towering water walls crashed together, pounding horses, chariots, and warriors into the sea floor. As witnesses to his power and wrath, they feared him.

When God instituted a system of law where every precise and strange detail pointed to his holiness, it was not to riddle them with more anxiety. It was a means to preserve them from it. The Law was the means to get rid of the sin that provoked his anger and provide fellowship between the human and the Divine the way he had instituted it in the beginning.

To host the Holy One, they would need to grasp the gravity of living with God. The straight measuring rod of his law continuously marked their failure to live a life straight enough to match.

The notable thing about this suffering woman is that she wasn't cursing the Law. She was abiding by it, trying to get clean so she could participate in corporate worship. Her condition wasn't sinful, but the blood was a reminder of the sinful world she lived in. A world where blood circulating inside a body pulses with life, nourishment, and cleansing. Blood outside the body startles, defiles, and signals death—a wage that must be paid. When Christ did for her what she had spent so long trying to do for herself, we can imagine she collapsed under the weight of worship.

Fellowship Restored. Life Renewed.

This woman didn't wait until she was healed to seek Jesus. When she went crawling to him, she was still bleeding and leading the way to the One whose blood gives life. Jesus has fulfilled the law. He has done for us what we cannot do for ourselves, even though we have tried so hard.

Hard Obedience

Sometimes we are the hemorrhaging, bleeding tears, bitterness, and rhetorical questions. Has hard obedience caused you suffering? Perhaps an illness has kept you from corporate worship. Maybe you've avoided a community of Christ followers for fear of your forgiven past being exposed. Maybe you've suffered at the hands of the church. Maybe you've been excluded from the healthy comforts of family. Perhaps your suffering is because you've tried your best to obey God.

Is God disappointed with you? Was your preparation wasted? Was service to others in the name of Christ in vain?

The answer is no—an emphatic no. To Jesus, the time was not lost. Your service was not squandered. Your preparation was not wasted. God looks into your heart, sees your suffering and your obedience. Your faith clings to Jesus. He has tethered your heart to his through Scripture heard long ago, a memory of his visible work in your life, or a promise from his word. Yours is childlike trust that he does all things well. Through a long silence, you clung to what you know of him without regular affirmations from a faith community or family. You hung onto him anyway. Asked from him anyway. You knew Jesus.

Even when we do not understand it, even though we lack the external marks of what humans normally applaud, faith that suffers and seeks Jesus because he is good is remarkable faith.

~

Oh Lord,

In the midst of great suffering I cannot understand why you sometimes restrain your powerful hand. I have waited long. Asking, listening, doubting, and finally forgetting to ask. Remind me that even in your silence, you see. You hear. You know.

Though I'd never choose suffering, you cultivate faith in the sacred soil of desperation. Your ways are not my ways.

I confess I've tried to clean myself up, scrub out the consequences, cover the signs of my sickness, but I've grown more sick and tired. I was stuck and you were silent.

Then you came offering to mend, liberate, and save. Believing you could do such things, I reached out to receive your offer.

While I was fitted with your righteousness, you contracted the stains of my sin. You suffered with it, died from it, and finally overcame it.

Thank you for hearing, for coming, for exchanging, for cleansing, for saving. I cannot help but worship.

Distant Faith

The Samaritan Leper

Now on his way to Jerusalem, Jesus traveled along the border between Samaria and Galilee. As he was going into a village, ten men who had leprosy met him. They stood at a distance and called out in a loud voice, "Jesus, Master, have pity on us!"

When he saw them, he said, "Go show yourselves to the priests." And as they went, they were cleansed.

One of them, when he saw he was healed, came back, praising God in a loud voice. He threw himself at Jesus' feet and thanked him—and he was a Samaritan.

Jesus asked, "Were not all ten cleansed? Where are the other nine? Has no one returned to give praise to God except this foreigner? Then he said to him, "Rise and go; your faith has made you well."

—Luke 17:11–19

He sat on the dank cave floor grasping the bleeding stump of an old man's wrist. With a thin piece of tree bark to protect his own fingers, he squeezed and plucked a slew of cactus spines from the wrist while his patient nodded off to sleep.

"Where did you get into these?"

He woke for a minute, irritated. "I don't know. Didn't see 'em until you did."

It was difficult to think of the old man as a friend. They were more of a functional necessity for each other. They'd started out rough and neither had been able to overlook a wrong in the miserable months that had followed. The day he joined them at the caves and saw the old man for the first time, it was as if his own death was staring him down. He staggered up the hillside that first day under the burden of a scant bundle of belongings and heavy losses. He stopped to take in the scene. At first he saw no movement except the wisps of smoke curling upward from several smoldering fires. The mouth of each cave was open. Its inhabitants were tucked inside and still as stones. At the sight of him they emerged like gravel tumbling down the slightest slope and cried in raspy voices over and over, "Unclean!"

The oldest of them moved along on the stumps of his wrists, his legs crossed in front of him and his feet long ago ground away by many a barefoot climb up and down the hill. Clothed in torn and filthy rags, nine men—or partial men—blended in with the brush and stones on the hillside. Some were missing fingers, some walked on infected heels, and one man had only a cavity where a nose had been. The sight and stench of decaying and infected flesh overcame him and he began to gag.

Observing his torn tunic and veil, the external warnings of an infected leper, one of the cave dwellers said, "You're joining us then?"

Still bent over with nausea, he nodded.

"You'll get used to it."

He couldn't imagine it. He removed the rag covering his face, wiped his mouth and cleared his throat. Covering his nose and mouth, he asked, "Is there a place for me?"

Upon hearing him speak, the old man laughed and replied, "Ah, doubly cursed. A Samaritan and a leper." He waved a wrist along the porous hillside. "Take your pick." That was the welcome they gave a foreigner, a half-blood Samaritan.

He reexamined the macerated wrist, and tossed it back in the old man's lap.

"Done already?" the old man spoke from his sleep.

Outside the cave and just down the hill a young woman hollered from the road and they looked to see who it was. "There are two loaves to share," she yelled and laid them on the ground.

The youngest of the ten lepers in the colony recognized his sister's voice and hurried out to see her from a distance. "Thank you! How is Mother?" he rasped. He was the youngest but leprosy had affected his voice more than it had for those who'd suffered longer.

"What's that?" she hollered back.

"Mother! How is Mother?"

"Not well. We have food, but she's not able to eat. I've brought you what is left."

He waved a sad acknowledgment, and she wiped her cheeks as she turned back toward the village.

He scrambled toward the loaves laid at the bottom of the hill, then unwrapped them and bit into a loaf on the way back up. The rest he begrudgingly handed to the Samaritan leper, who still had full use of both hands. He tore them into pieces and passed them to the others who had now swarmed around them at the mention of bread.

Before the woman was inside the gates of the village, the ten lepers sat in silence, scavenging crumbs out of their beards and savoring every tiny taste. "I want more." They all thought it. Only one was irritated enough to say it. What could any of them do? They passed the time telling cynical jokes, sarcastic riddles, and sometimes stories. Hunger was always the best time for stories about food. One of them began remembering. "I once saw a man feed thousands of people with just a few loaves of bread."

They all looked at him, waiting for the rest of the joke. He stared into the fire as though he were still at the place. "What are you talking about?" another asked in disbelief.

"His name was Jesus," he answered. "A large group of us heard him teaching and telling stories for three days on the other side of the river." He nodded straight down the road, toward the other side of the Jordan. "I'd never seen or heard anything like him. He just kept talking and teaching and answering questions." He shook his head to remember. "And the bread . . . it just kept coming."

They were each listening intently, as though still waiting for him to laugh at them for being so interested.

"They say he is the Son of God."

"Is that supposed to be the riddle?" one man asked.

"God has cursed us," said the old man. "What would we want with his Son?"

"God can curse as well as show mercy," replied the man without a nose.

"He's shown no mercy to you, has he?" The old man gestured toward the man's face.

The Samaritan searched each face and added, "There are some in Samaria who believe this Jesus is the Messiah..."

They all laughed. It was a stupid thing to say. He knew it. They would not take a Samaritan's report seriously.

He retreated to an outcropping of rock he'd claimed that first day. Here he was alone. The grassy place where he'd slept, sat, cried, and ate was now bare ground. He drew up his knees and buried his face in his arm to muffle the sobs. How many days until the numbing disease stole feeling from his fingers and toes? How many weeks until he slept too close to the fire and woke not to a searing burn, but to the stench of his burning hair and flesh? How many months of down the hill and back up before his feet were ground to infected nubs? He wished the numbing disease would affect his heart instead of his limbs. If only he could numb the pain of being outcast, alone, and bereaved—to stop dreaming of all he'd lost—especially his wife.

She had noticed it first in his beard. A tiny patch of graying whiskers just below his cheekbone. "So wise so soon?" she joked. He fingered the longest strands of beard and examined them. He was surprised. His father wasn't even gray, neither on his head nor his beard. When she noticed another graying patch of beard later that week, the teasing turned into questions. When a pink welt developed on his hand and the dark coarse hairs in it turned white, he left to visit their Samaritan priest.

Since the temple of Samaria lay in 160 years of rubble at the top of Mount Gerizim, the Samaritan priests worked and served closer to the cities. They practiced their rituals less formally than the Jewish variety, although they were no less determined to follow the Law of Moses.

As he entered the small stonewalled courtyard, the priest met him. Inside the makeshift temple sat the sacred law—a commonality between the Samaritan and Jewish priests, their common anchor, despite their differing practices. The priest took one look at his beard and welted hand, and prescribed two weeks of isolation to determine whether or not the disease on his skin was infectious.

After two weeks of torturous solitude, the priest's final examination revealed the worst. Leprosy, an infectious disease that seemed harmless at first. Flaking skin, falling hair, no pain at all. Eventually, though, the disease would spread from the skin, down inside the fingertips and hand, and eat away all the feeling. Without sensation his body received no internal signal of injury. Infection grew easily without the warning signs of pain. The infection was hardly any trouble until it began to carve away at the body; starting at the fingers, the toes, the nose, it worked its way further up and further in. It was a long and ugly, but physically painless death. Throughout the history of their ancestry it had been a sign of judgment for sin. Those with infectious diseases as well as sinful people were forced from the community and into the caves.

The priest recited his fate from the Law as though he was merely talking to the scroll: "The person with such an infectious disease must wear torn clothes, let his hair be unkempt, cover the lower part of his face and cry out, 'Unclean! Unclean!' As long as he has the infection he remains unclean." He stopped and looked directly at the trembling leper. "He must live outside the camp."

"Isn't there a recitation?" he interrupted. "A stone to touch or kiss? A sacrifice? Anything? I will do anything!" He fell to the ground toward the priest, who backed away.

"There is nothing. Leprosy is a divine curse. You have angered God. Only he can reverse it."

"But where shall I go? And what about my wife?"

"There is a colony of Jews who've been likewise cursed. They live buried in the caves running alongside our border with Galilee. You will find them."

"They are Jews! We have no dealings with them!"

"Leprosy is the great equalizer. They won't begrudge you a space. You've all sinned alike. Now, tear your clothing and use this to cover your face." The priest handed him a linen scrap that might well have been used to embalm the dead.

"But my wife," he whispered from behind his shabby veil. He had arrived home veiled and whispered through sobs, "Unclean!"

Devastated, she fell to the floor, shoulders heaving, gasping for air and inhaling dust. At the sight of his crying mother and disguised father, their little son began crying too, clawing at his mother for safety and comfort. All the sobbing had drawn the neighbors from both sides. They came running to the door. One woman remarked, "God in heaven! What's all the crying? You're both here! We thought there'd been a death!"

He turned to reveal his veiled face and torn tunic.

A howling jackal announced its dawn departure and woke the Samaritan leper from his recurring, real-life nightmare. He crawled out from the crag, and the early sun blinded him. He squinted toward the others. They never forbade him to join them, and they never invited either. The feelings were mutual, but loneliness was suffocating. One figure slumped toward the smoldering fire, blowing the ash and stirring the coals. On the road below he saw two men coming from the nearby village and a man with two pack mules coming from the other direction. Two of the lepers ambled down the slope just a bit toward the road and rasped together, "Unclean!" They were hardly noticed except for the mule, who slowed to see what creature made the indistinguishable noise. His master's whip sped him up again.

Not many people passed by in a day. Nearly every other day someone—a daughter, a sister, sometimes a mother—would leave a bundle at the bottom of the hill. Those who walked best took turns. They'd wave an acknowledgment and start toward the road. Their news was hollered to one another from a distance.

In the months since he'd arrived, the Samaritan leper found his place among the rest. He needed food and they needed his function. With all ten fingers still intact, he could tie a strip of dirty linen around a bloodied leg. When the moist wind snuffed out the fire, he could still strike the flint to light the kindling. They paid him in stale bread left by the roadside. It was an arrangement by necessity, and they tolerated one another. Leprosy was, as the old priest had said, the great equalizer. Still, the handicapped men each felt their own race was superior.

The sun was high and shone into the caves just a few feet, blinding them all as they sat and stared down the road. Just as he'd reached them, one man pointed a crooked finger down the road. "What's that?" he whispered.

Usually only a few villagers traveled to and from the village, and most often in small groups. Coming up the road toward the village was a group so large they filled the width of the road and spilled onto the roadsides. It was large enough to be the rebel zealots that gained momentum around the Jewish feasts. But the humming conversation lacked the angry shouts of disgruntled rebels. They were of all ages; women, men, and children talked, listened, and laughed. Someone would surely toss something their way. A loaf? A nearly empty sack of grain they were eager to lay down? They waited, watched, and wondered as the crowd came into view.

Then one leper stood abruptly and walked a few steps from the caves. "That's him." His tone alarmed them.

"Who?"

He pointed and whispered without turning back. "The teacher." They each strained to see. Another stood, and the old man maneuvered himself around the others to see for himself. "That's the man I saw breaking bread over and over."

The Samaritan studied his face and could see he was not joking. Each of the ten men were gradually maneuvering in front of one another to get a better view of the teacher—Jesus, who had fed thousands and some believed was the Messiah.

His robe flapped in the breeze and as he walked,

his hem dusted the ground then shook itself clean in the wind. He visited with the men surrounding him and turned when someone behind him spoke. Women carried babies and called to children who ran too far ahead. It was as if every happy Jew had been herded from the pastures of Galilee and were being led down this road by their rabbi Jesus.

Then, as if each leper decided it was his turn to descend the hill, they tumbled out of the caves, seeping from the hillside, tripping over rocks, wanting to be first. One by one, they made a hobbling ruckus. But not one of them was calling himself unclean. "Jesus!...Master!" Their raspy cries were barely distinguishable from the wind, so they cried out more with all the volume they could muster. Their cries muffled by dirty veils, their clothing almost indistinguishable from the drab brush, they were a masked and desperate mob. The Samaritan gained ground faster and hollered above the rest, "Jesus, Master, have mercy on us!"

Would Jesus, a Jewish rabbi, have mercy on him, a Samaritan? He stood at the base of the hillside, and maintained the required distance from the crowd on the road.

The rest of the lepers caught up. They were panting and bleeding. When Jesus looked up from his conversations, he saw them. *We are a desperate lot*, the Samaritan thought as he surveyed the crisp and lovely crowd surrounding Jesus. Nearly all had hair.

Jesus stopped and the crowd halted behind him. A woman swept up her son and buried him under her shawl. A startled little girl screamed and ran to her father. Jesus cupped his hands around his mouth, and in the wind they heard his answer. "Go and show yourselves to the priests!"

The lepers were befuddled. Did Jesus mean for them to go into the city? He gave no further explanation, so they all shuffled toward the village and the priest.

Wondering what a Jewish priest would do to him, the Samaritan rubbed his chin while he moved along with the others. As he did, he felt the thick stubble of a beard where only flaky, bare flesh had been. He stopped. He examined his hands. New skin replaced a scab where he'd ground his knuckles down striking the flint.

Behind him came loud crying. The old man was doubled over, examining his healed feet, gasping for air.

The Samaritan leper froze. Nine healed lepers bustled around him. Hollering and laughing, they rushed toward the village priests.

Though the Samaritan was healed, he would not be welcome in the village because he was not Jewish. The stunned crowd lingered in the road behind him with Jesus at the front. "It's him!" He ran toward Jesus. "You are the one! Praise be to God!" Throwing himself to the ground at Jesus' feet he cried, "Thank you! Jesus! Thank you for having mercy on me!" He buried his face in healed hands and felt the shelter of Jesus above him when he spoke.

"Now, weren't there ten men healed?"

The Samaritan nodded; the traveling crowd mumbled a collective yes.

"But the other nine . . . where are they?"

Jesus and the healed Samaritan leper both looked down the road toward the village. The other nine had disappeared inside the city gates. Jesus turned to the men and women following him. "Was no one found to give praise to God except this foreigner?"

No answer came from the stunned crowd, still reeling from their distant encounter with the lepers and shocked that their rabbi would accept this response from one they so disliked.

Jesus extended his hand to the weeping, cleansed Samaritan, who grasped it gladly. Jesus pulled him to his feet and said, "Stand up and go; your faith in me has saved you."

"Thank you," the Samaritan whispered again. He grasped Jesus' hand with both of his and stood to go home. He would tell his Samaritan family that Jesus was the one they had been waiting for. His healing would be the proof.

Far from Others, Far from God

All ten of the lepers, Jew and Samaritan, had been stripped of every privilege and dignity. Their only job was survival. It would have been difficult to wield a hammer or a plow with deteriorating hands and feet. Even if they could, no one would have bought their carpentry or crops because everything they touched, everything they had been close to, was contaminated. Not only was their disease contagious, it was also thought to be God's judgment for sin, and therefore spiritually contagious as well. Besides being judged as far from God, the Samaritan leper was distanced by the disease from everything familiar. He was an outsider who was met with undisguised hatred.

Cure for the Contagious

Though the Law of Moses provided for the cleansing of lepers, and allowed a lepers' court in the temple for those who had been healed, they understood a cure would only come by God's divine intervention. One did not simply "get over" leprosy as one would eventually "get over" a cold. Any hope the ten lepers had of returning to their former lives was completely dependent on Jesus being who they'd heard he was. They stood at a distance, as required by the Law, hoping that rumors about his miracles and divine power were true. When they saw Jesus, they didn't call out "unclean!" They called out for mercy.

Jesus saw them and his heart broke with compassion. They were harassed and helpless. Lost, confused, and distant, they appeared to Jesus as sheep without a shepherd (see Matthew 9:36). He came to seek and save and bring them near (see Luke 19:10).

Without explanation, he instructed them to do

what clean and healed lepers were supposed to do—
go to the priests. As they obeyed, he healed them—all
ten men at once. It was as if Christ placed ten excla-
mation marks at the end of the declaration he made
the last time he was in Samaria: I am the Messiah
you've been waiting for (see John 4:26).

Commendable Faith

All ten were healed, restored to their community,
arguably raised to life, in a physical sense. "God's grace
extends to all, but only some receive the gift of salva-
tion. That greater gift is received by faith, faith like
that of the Samaritan who comes to Jesus. Only he
among the ten walks away with a commendation that
explains why he is so blessed."[8] The other nine run
away so thrilled with the gift they forget the Giver.

When the Samaritan saw what Jesus had done, he
did not maintain his distance. He was compelled to
run to Jesus, the Great High Priest. Jesus performed
the healing that allowed the Samaritan to come near.
Jesus broke the dividing wall of hostility between Jew
and Samaritan with compassion and mercy. The distance between them became unnecessary. The veil

over the healed leper's face no longer separated his face from Christ. His gratitude springs from faith, which Jesus always sees. Jesus welcomes the Samaritan, saying, "Your faith in me has saved you."

A Spiritual Healing to Close the Distance

The thankful Samaritan leper is the spiritual model for all who have trusted Christ. Whether by prejudice, hate, rebellion, distraction, or doubt, we too were once far from him, distanced by the disease of sin. Sin separated us from his holiness, excluded us from the benefits of fellowship with him. God initiated a spiritual healing in us through Jesus when, like the Samaritan, we were foreigners to his kingdom (see Ephesians 2:12–13).

Even when we don't love each other—behaving toward one another like the Jews and Samaritans in Scripture—Jesus takes our leprous sin and gives us his holiness. We were once far off and, because of Jesus, we have been allowed to come near God. Christ's work tears down a wall of hostility between nations and makes us into one family in Christ (see Hebrews 7:19).

Christ's perfect life, credited to those who admit they need it, made us righteous. And "this righteousness is given through faith in Jesus Christ to all who believe" (Romans 3:22). On the day Jesus died, the thick, heavy veil in the temple that separated the holy from the sinful was no longer necessary. God tore it down to show us that in Christ we are welcome to approach him with bold confidence (see Hebrews 4:16).

Rewarded with Worship

Once Jesus has drawn us close, our glad impulse is to worship. Worship is the irrepressible outworking of a life changed by him. "God is the focus of worship, but we are its primary beneficiaries."[9] Worship and gratitude intertwine, and while we might think they are services we render to God, they are actually his reward to us. They are gifts by which God nurtures his relationship with us and evidence of remarkable faith.

Oh Lord,

While I was still far away, you made a way for me to come close to you. I was sinful and separated. You were holy and working to bring me back. In obedience to your father you accepted the consequences I deserved, and you gave me your perfect life to claim as my own.

You made me righteous. It doesn't seem right. It sounds like a scandal, but it was the only way. My disease of sin could only be cured by you.

Now that you have made me well and righteous, you have given unfettered access to your father, your friendship, and your spirit.

How can I thank you? I thank you with the gift of worship.

Panicked Faith

The Mother of a Demon-Possessed Girl

Leaving that place, Jesus withdrew to the region of Tyre and Sidon. A Canaanite woman from that vicinity came to him, crying out, "Lord, Son of David, have mercy on me! My daughter is demon-possessed and suffering terribly."

Jesus did not answer a word. So his disciples came to him and urged him, "Send her away, for she keeps crying out after us."

He answered, "I was sent only to the lost sheep of Israel."

The woman came and knelt before him. "Lord, help me!" she said.

He replied, "It is not right to take the children's bread and toss it to the dogs."

"Yes it is, Lord," she said. "Even the dogs eat the crumbs that fall from their master's table."

Then Jesus said to her, "Woman, you have great faith! Your request is granted." And her daughter was healed at that moment.

—Matthew 15:21–18
Parallel Passage: Mark 7:24–30

She carried her little girl down the slopes of her childhood hometown toward the Great Sea. The wind was strong, and the layered hems of her cloak made a dull crack with each gust. It whisked up the sand and pelted her skin, as if the gods of the sea were angry she had not brought her little girl sooner.

The salty air was good for weak children, she'd been told. It certainly had been for her as a child. She had run along the beaches, climbed mounds of sunbleached rocks, and collected every variety of seashell. She found them in the tide pools, on the beach, and wedged between rocks.

Shell collecting wasn't merely a pastime for her and her father. It was their job. The murex sea snail emitted a purple dye that was admired and in demand. To harvest it, workers from Tyre gathered murices by the bucket, dumped them in metal vats, crushed the snails to a pulp, and boiled them for days. The smell of rotting snails wafted up the cliffs and beaches and putrefied the air far inland. The stench was disagreeable, but it was a small inconvenience compared to the wealth it brought from kings and nations around the Great Sea. "I'd rather live in the stink of Tyre and have everything I want than to waste away in the fresh sea breeze of Sidon," her father had once said when she covered her mouth and gagged on the thick air.

It was true; they'd never lacked anything. Her father was in the most successful industry in Tyre, maybe the most successful on this side of the Great Sea. Ships from Egypt docked regularly to buy their purple dye as well as every sort of thing that could be dipped and colored in it. It was the color of a dark red wine. Unlike a stain of spilled wine, the dye extracted from the sea snails grew brighter and deeper with sunlight and time.

It was her joy, her entertainment, her education to clamor along with her father, finding shells, dropping them in his bucket, and occasionally stuffing one in the deep folds of her cloak to take home and keep in a jar of sea water. If she poked the little snail with a stick, he would emit the dark dye. Cloth, leather, stones, and sand dollars all begged to be decorated.

With drops of dye, she created rough imitations of the ornate carvings she saw on the temple of Melqart, Lord of Tyre. His temple stones and pillars had been carved with the familiar swirls of the various sea snails and images of the frightening seahorse upon which Melqart rode.

She had learned about Melqart from her father as they dropped the murices into buckets dragged through the sand. She heard the shells clank as he told her of the ancient temple of Melqart adorned by two pillars—one of gold and one inlaid with emeralds. It was said they gleamed and glittered in the sunlight and moonlight, drawing attention to the god of their city. She'd imagined their splendor and made drawings of the pillars.

Over time her sea snail's water would evaporate, and too much salt would begin to poison it. When he began to stink, she would throw him back into the sea for Melqart to fix, and fish out another with a new jar of water.

She stood at the edge of the sea now with her daughter sleeping. The mist from the breaking waves dampened her feet and face. The air was salty, and though spring was gone, the stench from the boiled murices lingered as if the porous cliffs had soaked it up.

How long must we stand here and breathe the salty air? she wondered. *How often should I come?* Staring into the water searching for signs of those demolished pillars, she wondered if it was Melqart's power that comes up from the sea, or if the air itself made a child strong. She looked down at her daughter, still sleeping, apparently unaffected by either.

She sat down on the white sand and crushed shells until the sun started to dip into the sea. A fleet of ships, with the goddess Astarte leading from the bow, docked and the shipmen disembarked. They hurried up the beach to eat, drink, and revel in the freedom of being on land.

When they were mostly gone, she headed for home. With her daughter's head resting on her shoulder, she hiked away from the old island city, over the causeway toward the mainland of Tyre. The walk was always a reminder of Tyre's enemies and wars. Alexander the Great had led his war machines to trample over the old island. Then he connected their island city to the mainland by filling up the narrowest part of the sea with the rubble of all he destroyed, creating a causeway that had, for centuries, opened their region to Greek thinkers, Roman soldiers, priests of Greek and Roman gods, and many wealthy traders.

Growing up in Tyre, with so much attention from far-off places, meant every vendor's booth was filled with foreign treasures for a young lady to see and love. Before long, she'd seen plenty of money and trade, shipmen and soldiers, and had a daughter of her own. She shifted her daughter onto her other shoulder as she passed under the Roman arches that marked the way through town. Finally, back at her father's house, she tucked her darling into bed to sleep some more.

Month after month, walk after walk, the putrefied sea breeze had not strengthened her daughter. She knew she must try something else. Egypt had Pharaoh, Greece had Zeus, Rome had Jupiter, Israel had Yahweh, Sidon had Astarte, and Tyre had Melqart, the Lord of the City. She was frightened by the gods. They were terribly unpredictable. They could be convinced and cajoled by proper gifts. What was a proper gift to curry favor from the gods? No one knew for sure. In ancient days, women gave their children to Melqart in a fire to satisfy his anger or solicit help. She just needed him to make her daughter strong. It was a small favor for a god like Melqart.

Her daughter, at this age, should be walking on the beaches shoving every sandy shell in her pockets, but the little girl could only sit. She should be talking and laughing, but she mostly slept. She should be gobbling up every kind of fruit from the market, but she drank only milk and water and had to be fed the mashed fruit.

She could not, would not, give Melqart her daughter. She could not toss her little girl to him as though she was a murex for Melqart to fix. Instead, she would bring other sacrifices he would like. She had plenty.

One afternoon, with her daughter curled up on the bed sleeping, she began to sort through her father's treasures and her own. She dug into a chest of Tyrian coins, the standard in Phoenicia. Four handfuls filled a leather bag. She had decorated the bag herself by pressing the spines of a shell into the leather and filling the indentations with purple dye from her sea snail. The design appeared as a carefully arranged smattering of coagulate blood, and Melqart might be pleased with the likeness of blood. She fingered a silver ring, a gift from her father. The inset jade stone ran from the base of her finger to the knuckle and was carved with the most ghastly image of Melqart's monstrous seahorse. She never liked the ring or its raised image, but she wore it occasionally to please her father and Melqart. It might please him more to have it, she thought, and she slipped it on.

It made good sense. The gods would not perform favors for anyone who did not leave an acceptable gift. She brought from her treasures all he might love. None of them were especially dear to her, but they were all of highest quality, originality, and to his liking, she thought. She pulled the strap of the leather bag over her head and situated it on her shoulder.

Though her daughter was weak and thin, she was still growing and it took both arms to carry her. She swaddled her frail girl close to her with a sash to keep her secure. Her head rested against her mother's chest, and her legs dangled near her mother's waist. She smiled and slept as her mother carried her toward Melqart's temple. She was calm and lovely, weak and tired.

At the base of the stairs approaching the temple grounds a woman whispered to every passerby: "Melqart cannot help you." Taking the briefest opportunity to speak with anyone who hesitated as they climbed the stairs to the temple, she said: "There is a descendant of King David in Galilee who can."

The mother was startled. Who says such a thing,

and at the stairs of his temple where Melqart might hear! The whispering woman's words were urgent but not frenzied. Most ignored her, so when the little girl's mother showed a moment of interest, she offered, "I will take you to him."

The mother felt strangely hopeful. It seemed unwise, maybe even dangerous. Cautious not to offend Melqart, confident she'd brought the right gifts and sacrifices for him, she looked the woman in the eye. The woman spoke louder: "I have been to Jerusalem and seen him." The mother turned away and pretended not to hear. Melqart was king of Tyre; what could a man from the regions of Israel have that Melqart did not? She boosted her little girl up. "He has healed the sick. Completely healed them." The mother ignored the offer. "He is the Son of God," she called out from behind. All the Roman rulers claimed to be sons of the gods. Now apparently a Galilean made that claim. She continued up the stairs and neared the height of Melqart's temple.

The priest accepted the gift on Melqart's behalf. Sliding the ring onto his own finger, he admired the carved image for a moment, then emptied the leather pouch heavy with coins. They rolled onto the table and he poured handfuls onto his brass scale, counting and measuring, examining each treasure and assigning a value. Finally he read an incantation, touched her little girl's head, and dismissed them.

"What shall I expect? Will she be strong?"

"Never speak back to a priest unless you have favors to offer!" He shooed her out of the temple with a scolding. "And never question the gods!"

Her daughter was agitated that night. She thrashed in her sleep and wailed. By the morning of that dreadful night, she knew Melqart had tricked her. He had taken her best gifts and made her daughter strong, yes, but he had changed her into a frightened girl who gnawed on her own knuckles until they cracked and bled.

Month after month the mother lost sleep, cursed the gods, and finally returned to the temple to try again. *This time I will not question Melqart*, she thought. *I will be silent before the priest.* She was silent and did not question, but no matter what she brought, no matter what she did or did not do, Melqart continued his trick. Each time she visited, her daughter became stronger, and less like herself. With her increased strength she began to run toward the sea every time she smelled the stench of the sea snails boiled by the dyers. She tried to throw herself in. When her mother confined her to the house for her own safety, she clung to pillars and furniture in dark corners.

Still the mother returned to Melqart's temple, with larger, more precious gifts: purple silk; a jeweled statuette of Melqart's mother, the goddess Astarte; and a jar of Sidonian coins with her image stamped on every one. Each time she returned to the temple, the curious woman was there offering to take a tortured soul for a day's trek into Galilee. "He has driven out demons," she heard her say. "He has made the lame strong."

The mother was hesitant to believe. Melqart had claimed the same, and look what he had done. He had proven cunning and deceptive. He could not be trusted. He required much, and tricked in return. She hated him. Now her daughter was more a beast than a child. She still did not speak. She only screamed and cried. She could stand, but she could also run away. And her strength! She had become so unnaturally strong that her mother could hardly manage her. Whatever Melqart had put inside her daughter would drive her into dark places to cling to anything that could not be moved: a narrow pillar in the corner of the room, a wooden rack anchored in the stone wall, the furnishings carved of stone. All the cajoling and reason could not convince her to let go. It was as if she could not let go if she'd wanted to. Though her mother tried to free her, she could not pry her daughter's little fingers from whatever they clutched without snapping them right in two. When she was not anchored overnight to stationary pieces, she was running about, sniffing like a dog for every shard of something sharp: broken pottery on the road, a glass bead dropped on the floor and split in two, even the spines and spires of her mother's collection of shells. When she got hold of them, even for a moment, she would scratch her own flesh. The beautiful treasures the mother had collected became potential dangers, reasons to panic, and fuel for hate. Her days were spent restraining her daughter.

Only when she led her into the low mountainous border of the region, into the fresh smell of cedar, away from the sea, did her daughter ever seem to calm. The cedars were thick and always green, blotting out the sun and giving shelter from the winds off the sea. They could rest against the trunks, listen for mice skittering over roots, and occasionally catch a glimpse of one in a hurry to nibble a large seed into edible pieces.

The calm never lasted, and she could not live in the mountains alone with her girl. The forest was cold and frightening. No matter how hard she tried to stay, she always returned to the comforts of her father's house and the tortures of her demonized daughter.

Home again after one such morning among the cedars, she poured a drink for the two of them that slipped from her grip and crashed to the floor. She rushed for rags and returned to see her daughter clutching a shard of glass, jabbing designs into her forearm. When she had finally wrestled with her to pry it from her fingers, and gently wiped the injury, she saw the rude and jagged sketch of Melqart's sea monster on her forearm. She screamed.

With nothing to occupy her scabbed hands, the little girl wrapped herself around a pillar in a dark corner of the house and would not—could not—let go. She would stay there all day and into the night, crying, occasionally screaming, and immovable.

The bloody sketch on her daughter's arm summoned her to return to Melqart's temple. He had stolen her wealth and destroyed her daughter. What else did he want? She gathered gifts from her depleted supply and arrived at the temple tired and sick.

She stumbled up the stairs and noticed the happy ambassador of the Galilean was gone. She heard no stories of the lame who now walked. No hope was spoken, no mention of one who could heal and drive out demons. She scanned the busy road to and from the temple and saw no one interrupting travelers with eager announcements. An elderly man crouched near the place where the woman always stood. His long white beard rested on his knees, drawn close to his chest.

"Where is she?" the mother asked him bluntly.

"She has a guest," he replied with gravel in his voice, "but she will return when he leaves." He seemed to know exactly whom she asked about.

"Where does she live?"

"On the main road, through the arches. Near the border of Tyre and Galilee."

Galilee. A guest. She startled herself with the thought. She was already in such poor favor with Melqart, she needed to bring him gifts, yet she could not ascend the temple stairs. She turned and scampered down.

The road was familiar and heavily traveled. Many came to Tyre by the sea. Nearly everyone who came by land went under the Roman arches and over their aqueducts. Today it seemed they had all come at the same time. She brushed the flanks of musky horses as she wove her way through the crowd. The smell of shorn sheep was thick as she hurried past the wool houses. Beyond the arches the road was dotted with houses along both sides, spread farther apart the farther she went. The road was level and less obstructed, so she began to run. She was breathing hard. *What on earth am I doing?* she scolded herself. Running from everything she knew, she rushed toward the hope of an uncertain rumor. Would an Israelite care for a Tyrian? Their countries had centuries of history filled with wars. To the Israelites, Tyrians were unclean. To them she was merely a dog who couldn't garner favor from her own city's god.

Why did that happy woman come to Melqart's temple every day without an offering? Without fear she turned his patrons away from him to the son of an ancient Israelite king. If she found him, she would appeal to him as such. She consoled herself with shaky encouragement and found herself wiping tears.

Like a Roman soldier, she peered into windows as if every house was her concern and her business.

Looking for the woman, and hoping her guest might be the one she'd spoken of, she stopped at every house. Then she saw her, tossing out a washbasin of dirty water, and hurrying back into her house. The mother ran the distance to the house, and straight up to the door. She heard the voices of men who mumbled and laughed, and she recognized the woman's voice: "More bread?"

She pounded the door with her fist and yelled, "I need your help!"

The voices quieted. No one came to the door. She pounded again. Her voice cracked with the long-suppressed cries of a broken heart. "I heard you in there! Please!" Did they not hear? She screamed to make sure, "Son of David! Have mercy on me!" She wiped her nose and tears on her sleeve, then held her breath to listen.

"We're here to rest," a man inside said.

"I'm begging!" She pounded again and pressed her face to the crack of the door. "Please! Help me! My daughter…she is suffering terribly! I think it's a demon. I think Melqart did it to her. I think I…"

The door remained closed, and she heard another man say, "Just help her and then send her away or she'll keep screaming and you'll be exposed. Everyone will know you're here. The rest of the region will be lined up at this door, and you'll have no rest at all."

"Yes!" she screamed. "I will go away, but I need you to come and get that thing out of her!" She pounded on the door again then. It opened, and she was face-to-face with the woman from the temple. "He's here, isn't he! Your friend from Galilee?" Inside the house a man walked toward her. He was not a frightening god with lightning bolts and a sea monster. He looked terribly ordinary. Nothing about him looked like the gods she knew. He could have been a neighbor.

"I was sent for the lost sheep of Israel," he said.

Falling to her knees she buried her face in her hands. "I know! But Lord...help!"

"First let the children eat all they want. It is not right to take the children's bread and toss it to their dogs."

"Of course not, Lord, but even the little dogs belong to the master of the house. And they are fed by the crumbs the children drop under the table. Please..."

Jesus bent down, lifted her chin, and looked into her eyes. "Oh, dear woman"—he paused and smiled—"you have great faith."

She wiped her face with her sleeve again and nodded.

"For such a reply, you may go."

"Please, don't dismiss me..."

"Friend, your request is granted. The demon has left your daughter. I have done it."

His face was as serious as hers. She detected no trickery or sly bargain in his voice, just a declaration, and she believed him. Scrambling to her feet, she grabbed his hand and kissed it.

She ran the entire distance to her father's house, panting and wondering. Inside, her daughter was not anchored to the pillar where she'd left her. She was gone. Running from room to room she found her lying in her bed, resting peacefully. She fell to her knees by the bed, and her daughter's eyes flickered open. Sitting up in her bed, she reached for her mother and smiled.

"Mama."

"Yes, baby?" She covered her own mouth so she didn't startle her with crying.

"I'm hungry."

She gathered her girl into her arms and wept fresh tears forced out by gratitude and worship. Then she guided her daughter to the kitchen, lifted the linen from the loaves on the table, and tore off a piece of bread for each of them. As they ate, an abundance of crumbs sprinkled on the table and scattered on the floor.

The Divine Collision of the Rejected Ones

Jesus taught, healed, and drove out evil spirits in Israel—his homeland. Despite the miracles, signs, and wonders he did in Israel, "He came to his own, and his own people did not receive him" (John 1:11, ESV). So he left there for a while to rest from his work and their exhausting rejection, and went to the border regions of Tyre and Sidon, a pagan region north of Galilee on the Mediterranean Sea.

In Tyre he might have been mobbed with the glad welcome of many who needed help. Word of his miracles had spread, and the people in this region were as lost as Israel. However, he had planned to keep his presence a secret in order to rest.

Jesus' miracles did not offend the Tyrians; instead, they were intrigued by them. They would learn that Christ was not sent to be one of many gods, he was sent as the exact representation of the One and Only

God (see Hebrews 1:3). Christ was called to minister to those who would reject him. He came to those who would scoff at his divine title, who would continually attribute his miracles to the work of the devil. The sick and needy in Israel, as well as the bewildered and hopeful foreigners from countries around the Mediterranean, came to Jesus with a hunger for a powerful and compassionate God. Many were healed, freed, and utterly changed. Upon Christ's instruction they returned to their homes. Some returned to Tyre. Likely the woman at Melqart's temple was one of them.

The mother was a worshipper of the false gods. She gave and they took. She pleaded and they tricked. She came but they rejected her. So God appointed a divine collision of a panicked woman rejected by her tricky "gods" and the Savior rejected by his people.

As hungry dogs can sniff out the buried bone, and hungry people cannot rest until they're fed, she came crying for mercy. Her plea for mercy recognized that Jesus is the authority who can decide to grant mercy or not.

She heard he was different, a kind master, so if she must sit under the table, as a little pet of the family, at least she would belong to a good God. It is the sentiment of the Psalmist who says to God, "Better is one day in your courts than a thousand elsewhere; I would rather be a doorkeeper in the house of my God than to dwell in the house of the wicked" (Psalm 84:10).

She humbly trusts Jesus—who does not steal, but gives, who does not destroy but restores, who does not kill, but offers himself as the Bread of Life. She is the willing recipient of anything he would offer her, whether it be a day in his courts, a position as a doorkeeper, or crumbs from his table.

Jesus does not refuse a broken and contrite heart. The mother knew her need and believed that any mercy he supplied would satisfy and deliver! Jesus saw it in her heart, but the others heard it by her reply, "Yes, Lord, but even the dogs eat the crumbs that fall from their master's table." Her words are proof of something unusual in her heart. That is why Jesus remarks, "Oh, woman, you have great faith!"

Panicked faith does not demand delicacies from the hand of Christ, but willingly accepts what appear to be leftovers, simply because they fall from his hand.

Leftovers for Life

Just as a dog sniffs out a trail of crumbs and follows them to their source, so the woman finds that what she thought were crumbly leftovers are actually the overflow of what Jesus gives in abundance. "I am the bread of life," Jesus said. "Whoever comes to me will never go hungry, and whoever believes in me will never be thirsty" (John 6:35).

While the priest of the false god stole her sacrifice, Jesus took away her suffering. Instead of destroying her, he destroyed her record of sin and guilt. Instead of death, he offered himself as the way to eternal life.

From Panicked Faith to Megafaith

Whether we will admit it or not, we have all worshipped something or someone other than our One True God.

False gods are the agents of the enemy. He prowls around looking to steal, kill, destroy, and devour, but he is not principled. He does not care if the method of destruction is pretty, or accepted, or even applauded.

As long as it destroys, Satan is satisfied. Modern false gods don't appear in a temple with pillars, so we don't always recognize them until we find ourselves suffering at their hands and starving for satisfaction.

Here is the good news of the gospel. Jesus redeems our panic and uses it to drive us to himself for relief. Panicked faith is not a tidy, demure, polite proposition as if to say, "I'm sorry to interrupt you, Jesus. I know you have important work to do for others, but I need just a small favor. If you can't grant it, no problem. I'm sure someone else can help."

The panic has driven us to him because no one else can help. Panicked faith is loud and urgent, desperate and scared. It interrupts and it disturbs. Panicked faith does not defend its position but declares its willingness to accept whatever Christ will offer; even a particle of his goodness is welcome.

Panic is not what moves Jesus to action. Loud urgency is simply the overflow of the repentant heart. Jesus gives grace to the person with a humble heart. Though the past can't be undone, we believe he can redeem and restore it anyway.

That is the faith Jesus commends. In the Greek language it is megafaith. In popular vernacular it's jumbo, epic, whopping faith.

Surprisingly this example of great faith is an invitation to eat the crumbs that inevitably lead to the abundant, sustaining source—Jesus, the Bread of Life.

Idols in Disguise

The idol of image—looking good.

The idol of false relaxation by numbing substances—feeling good.

The idol of comparison—focusing on the shortcomings of others to distract us from ourselves.

The idol of amusement—overloading our minds with "how-tos," "to-dos," or "must-haves."

The idol of chronic rushing—do, achieve, perform.

All of these are acceptable and addictive acts of worship directed toward false gods. When we realize our false gods of comfort have robbed us, destroyed relationships, and are leading us to sickness, we can run to Jesus! We must run to him sweaty and panting, screaming for rescue from the demands of abusive false gods. To come to him panicked, without depending on anything we've done, is remarkable faith.

If we have trusted Christ, if we have believe the gospel, if we have recognized him as the true God—the life giver and the Bread of Life—then we know he does not limit us to crumbs.

~

Dear Lord,

I confess I have loved a hundred other things more than you. I have chased after them as though they would save and give me peace. So many of them are good gifts like family, food, beauty, calling, even ministry. But when I treat them as "gods" to be worshipped, instead of gifts to be received, I find they take from me more than I can give. I end up worried and panicked. My joy is gone and I am driven to you in despair.

Remind me that your gifts are meant to point me to you as the Giver. Teach me to receive your rescue, help, and peace instead of searching for it in other places. Show me the crumbs of your abundant grace, which you have scattered around me that point me always back to you.

Defiant Faith

Blind Bartimaeus

As Jesus approached Jericho, a blind man was sitting by the roadside begging. When he heard the crowd going by, he asked what was happening. They told him, "Jesus of Nazareth is passing by."

He called out, "Jesus, Son of David, have mercy on me!"

Those who led the way rebuked him and told him to be quiet, but he shouted all the more, "Son of David, have mercy on me!"

Jesus stopped and ordered the man to be brought to him. When he came near, Jesus asked him, "What do you want me to do for you?"

"Lord, I want to see," he replied.

Jesus said to him, "Receive your sight; your faith has healed you." Immediately he received his sight

and followed Jesus, praising God. When all the
people saw it, they also praised God.

—Luke 18:35–43
Parallel passages: Matthew 20:29–34,
Mark 10:46–52

Bartimaeus crouched, dusting the ground with his
fingers, searching. The sun was already warming his
back, and he would be the last one down the hill.
He frantically raked his fingers through the dirt and
gravel until finally he found his sandals. He sat and
tied the leather straps. He felt for his wadded cloak,
shook it out, and draped it around his shoulders. He
was never without this cloak. In summer it was his
pillow; in the mild Jericho winter, his light blanket;
and every day, his collection basket. He could occasionally go without his sandals when he misplaced
them, but he could never do without his cloak. He
inched his way down the slope toward the road where
he could already hear the earliest travelers exiting the
city on their way to Jerusalem for Passover. Their post
was the only byway from Jericho to Jerusalem.

The feast of all Jewish feasts was just a week
away. The travelers were especially charitable, and

Bartimaeus feared his tardiness would deny him the advantage of begging from the most eager pilgrims. The trick was to sit by the road near the city gate in front of the many other beggars, so the first gifts might fall to him. Yet he could not sit so near the city gate that his grubby presence would surprise and offend travelers. Today, he'd spent so much time searching for his sandals that he didn't have a choice. *I ought to start leaving them on at night*, he thought as he scraped his way down the hill.

The noises became clearer as he neared the street. Shepherds shouted as sheep bawled and scampered in the road. The drone accompanying the noise was the daily mournful choir of a hundred other invalids begging. They beat on metal scraps, clicked sticks together, and shook pebbles inside pottery—a vigorous racket to gain attention. They cried for help, food, money, a kind word, but received them in scant portions.

He swept his sandals over his chosen plot of roadside to scatter sharp gravel, then eased himself to the ground. Swinging his cloak from off his back, he draped it over his lap, forming a makeshift basket to catch food or coins. He'd rather have food. Coins were tough to distinguish and keep track of.

To spend them meant a journey inside the city walls, where he was at the mercy of every dishonest vendor. The smaller coins he kept in a scrap of cloth tied to his belt on the left and the larger in a scrap tied to the right. If he couldn't tell immediately what kind of coin it was, he left them in his cloak drawn across his lap where they first landed, until he could slowly run his finger over the raised ridges on each side to determine where it ought to go.

Being tossed a piece of bread, even if it was stale, was much easier. It would ease his hunger and decrease his collection. A scrap of crust left in his lap might suppress the generous impulse of a sympathetic traveler. He'd eat it on the spot before anyone could steal it if he happened to doze off. With food, he didn't have to leave his post or discover what coins he carried. Stale bread, crunchy dates, even cheese crusted in dust were preferable to sorting coins and dealing with the market thieves.

He settled next to a fellow beggar and they called out together, "Alms for the poor?"

Polite conversation between two women in the street caught his attention. Their footsteps passed and nothing landed in his lap. "What was she saying?" his friend asked. They'd been privy to many private conversations. Their poverty disguised their intelligence, and people talked freely.

"Something about the king." Bartimaeus shivered even in the warmth of the sun.

"He's gone to Jerusalem for the summer, hasn't he?"

"Several weeks ago, I'd say." Herod was a volcano spewing hot violence to anyone who threatened his power or his purse.

They were quiet for a moment, offering silence as a memorial to what had happened the last time King Herod had passed by. They remembered the jangle of regal tack and hooves. All the beggars had hushed themselves. Seizing the opportunity, one eager beggar had cried out for money. Instead of plinking coins, they had heard a blunt thud and a crying groan from the uninformed victim. In wordless unison the terrified beggars had scrambled away, colliding as they fled. Bartimaeus had clawed and stumbled up the hill, as if escaping a hissing adder licking at his heels. He had finally slammed into the rocky wall of his den and slumped to the floor in the safety of his cave where no king would contaminate himself. By the next morning, hunger overpowered fear and the beggars crept back to the roadside. One of them tripped over the limp body; by evening they had bartered for the clothes of the disrobed dead man.

More footfalls broke their silent memorial and they called out again. Nothing. "We're too far from the gate," Bartimaeus complained. "I'm keeping my sandals on tonight!" A few bleating lambs scampered by and he instinctively covered his head and bent over his lap. In a herd, lambs were neither nimble nor careful. A young shepherdess called the startled sheep and they trotted by while her footsteps grew louder. Bartimaeus and his friend called out toward her, "A piece of bread for the blind?"

She did not answer, but she stopped.

Lambs jostled nearby, their humid panting warmed his cheek and their musk thickened the air. Sensing her youth he prodded, "A coin then? You'll sell your lambs easily in Jerusalem. Can you part with a few coins for a man who's never had a hardworking daughter like you?"

She said nothing, but Bartimaeus heard the soft slap of a leather strap and then shifting cloth.

"You won't have a use for coins until you get to Jerusalem."

Something heavy dropped in his lap. He grabbed

it and held it to his nose. It was a barley loaf. "Shhh," she said.

He was ashamed he had manipulated her youth. "May God give you joy for your kindness," he whispered.

A gruff voice hollered from the city gate, and the young shepherdess called back, "Here I am, Father. I found the lambs. They were just startled." She hurried away from the two blind beggars.

"Did you get a whole loaf?" his friend asked.

"Yes"

"Me too."

A steady stream of travelers passed throughout the morning. Bartimaeus ate half his barley loaf and shoved the rest under his cloak to make his poverty obvious. Another herd tapped out a calm trotting rhythm, indicating an experienced shepherd, or perhaps several. He strained to discern their mood, but the crunching gravel, occasional bleating, and the added jangle of tambourines and singing made it difficult to sort the hoofbeats from the footfalls. Before he could call out, the herd and its shepherds had passed, and his chest went cold with lost opportunity.

He tuned his senses toward louder music and

singing. Such a large and jovial group was a treasury begging to be relieved of its weight! It sounded larger than he remembered King Herod's entourage, but without the synchronized severity. This was a happily disorganized mass. Women sang familiar songs accompanied by their clinking finger cymbals. Mothers called after children, men discussed selling lambs in Jerusalem. The sounds were familiar, but the size of the group was like nothing he had ever heard. So many at one time. Bartimaeus feared his pleas would be drowned in the surge of Passover celebration.

The first part of the large crowd tromped past him. The road was so full, they'd begun stepping on the edges of his cloak, and he felt it being tugged from his lap. He scooted back from the tromping party, resituated his cloak, and shouted, "Hey! What's happening?"

He received no answer. He pressed one ear into the cacophony and then the other. Garments whisked the air and a man-made breeze cooled his face. He shouted up again.

"What is going on? Who is this?"

"It's Jesus of Nazareth passing by," a voice answered.

"Jesus of Nazareth!" His friend echoed his astonished thoughts aloud.

The joyful crowd was headed to Jerusalem for Passover. Of course! Merchants had spread news that Jesus caused commotion in the temple and quarreled with religious leaders. They had also brought stories of his healings! Hardly a traveler failed to mention Jesus of Nazareth! They either cursed or praised him.

Bartimaeus' heart pounded in his ears.

Most recently he heard rumors that Jesus had brought a dead man back to life. Ancient prophets had raised dead men, but no one had claimed to see such things until now. Travelers from Jerusalem spoke of a blind man who had begged near the temple since childhood. Jesus of Nazareth had opened his eyes on the Sabbath!

Israel's prophets and songs foretold that the Son of David, when he came, would bring good news, bind up the brokenhearted, free prisoners, and release captives from darkness. Bartimaeus grew frantic with hope. *Jesus! He can do it. He has done it.*

The enthusiastic crowd seemed to be swelling. Dust swirled thick into his nose and lungs, and once again he felt his cloak being tugged into the street.

He snatched it up and stuffed the fabric and contents completely into his lap. He turned his face left then right listening for a prominent voice. He heard none. "Jesus!" he hollered. He waited. "Jesus! Have mercy on me!" The only answer was the din of the lively crowd. Bartimaeus grabbed his friend's arm. "Together!" he shouted.

They cried louder searching for the direction in which to call, "Lord! Have pity on us!"

"Shut up!" someone yelled.

"I won't!" he growled in defiance.

"Just hush!" said another, followed by a mass shushing. "Don't you know who is passing by? Be quiet!"

It was all the confirmation he needed. It was Jesus! Bartimaeus was nearly bouncing on the ground. He screamed, "Jesus! Son of David, have mercy on me! Now!"

The scuffling feet slowed and the crowd calmed. Bartimaeus took full advantage of the lull and drew in his breath to scream again, when a man standing over him said, "Hey, there. Cheer up. He's calling for you to come…on your feet now."

Bartimaeus flung his wadded cloak with all its tiny treasure to the ground. He scrambled to his feet and listened carefully for a call he had not heard. Arms stretched stiffly in front of him, he pressed into the crowd. A man took hold of his elbow. "This way." Bartimaeus clung to the stranger's hand on his arm. He felt the murmuring bodies recede wherever the guide led. Then they stopped. "These were the ones screaming for you, Jesus." The guide released his elbow.

"What do you want me to do for you?" His voice was calm and certain. He did not scold Bartimaeus for screaming above the celebrating crowd. He issued an invitation. Bartimaeus was quaking yet unafraid.

"Lord"—he swallowed and steadied his voice to match his hope—"I want to see."

It was an obvious and audacious request. He felt almost foolish, except that Jesus of Nazareth could grant it! The wind through the palms, the squawk of overhead wrens, and the bustling animals and children, were all he heard in response. Then calloused, warm hands brushed grit from Bartimaeus' forehead and rested for a moment on his eyelids.

With fierce compassion Jesus spoke again. "Receive your sight." When Jesus removed his hands, Bartimaeus opened his eyes. The painful light of the blinding sun lit up his mind. Instinctively he pressed the ball of his hand into his eyes and rubbed out the sun. Peeking through the cracks of his fingers, he saw a bearded man squinting and smiling at him. "Your faith has healed you," he said.

Bartimaeus blinked over and over. Slowly, then fast. Light flashed in and out. He scanned the faces surrounding Jesus. Some smiled, some stared with mouths agape. Someone was crying, as was Bartimaeus. With teary vision, Bartimaeus looked at the sobbing man. He was draped in rags with bits of food and straw tangled in his beard. Tears trickled down his weathered cheeks. Though the sight was unfamiliar, Bartimaeus recognized the cry. It was his friend. He and his friend stood in contrast to the crowd of men who sported neatly trimmed beards, hemmed cloaks, and freshly oiled hair.

Bartimaeus grabbed his friend's sleeve and pulled him to the ground beside him. They knelt before Jesus, thanking him, praising God, looking up at him and bowing their heads again, every word of praise punctuated by tears. What had previously been only textures and noises now had color and depth. Jesus filled in the sensory gaps and gave not only vision, but a face-to-face encounter with the merciful Son of David himself. It was immeasurably more than all the blind beggar had asked or imagined.

Smiling, Jesus offered a hand to each, grasped them both, and pulled them to standing. As Jesus turned again toward Jerusalem, Bartimaeus and his friend fell in step beside him. Watching his every move and expression, they followed him, with no thought of an abandoned cloak, scattered coins, and a half-eaten barley loaf.

The singing began again, enlivened by awe for the One who led them.

The Sacred Gifts of Affliction

This blind man and his friend would be the first to admit the gifts offered by blindness, poverty, and affliction are scant and infrequent. *Bartimaeus* translated actually means "son of Timaeus," and we have no historical or biblical clues as to who his blind friend was or what he was named. Fumbling to survive and plagued by uncertainty, these blind beggars depended on handouts they couldn't see. But there are a few advantages of being a blind beggar, although such gifts are unwanted and disguised.

The Gift of Undeniable Need

The blind beggar had the advantage of knowing his inescapable need. Affliction drove him to the roadside to beg for crumbs of survival, to listen for any hope of healing. Because of his blindness, he saw—perhaps more clearly than others—his desperate need for intervention, help, and healing.

The Gift of Unashamed Receiving

Inescapable need and peace with a lifestyle of utter dependence has another advantage. Blind beggars are accustomed to receiving. The crowd wanted him to stop asking, but Jesus called him to come and receive. Bartimaeus had the uncommon habit of making obvious requests for help and eagerly accepting what was offered.

The Gift of Being Unaccustomed to Repayment

He also had the advantage of being unaccustomed to repayment. He was not used to paying back or proving his usefulness. Everything he owned or consumed had been given to him. He had no thought of repaying the giver, earning the gift by working it off, or deserving anything that was tossed his way.

The Gift of Uncommon Freedom

A lifetime marked by desperate need, unabashed receiving, and inability to repay had also gifted him with uncommon freedom. Unshackled by the restraints of polite society, he was used to defying social protocol. He had no reputation to maintain, no family legacy to uphold, no employer to honor, and no one to impress. He had nothing to lose by crying out loudly to Jesus and defying those who would hush him.

The Gift of Irresistible Desire

After the healing, Jesus surprisingly does not command Bartimaeus to follow him. He says to him, "Go your way. Your faith has made you well" (Mark 10:52, ESV).

The formerly blind beggar had nothing valuable to pack. Nothing valuable tethered him to Jericho. He was unfettered by material or social trappings. When a blind beggar is saved, he wants to go where his Savior is going.

Accompanied by a fresh love, zeal, and devotion for Christ, he followed him all the way to Jerusalem for Passover. Bartimaeus would smell the sacrificial smoke at the temple, taste the lamb and the bitter herbs of the Passover meal, then along with his first sights of the Passover celebration, he would see his Savior beaten, bloodied, crucified, and finally risen to life. What an extraordinary and traumatic week for an inexperienced disciple.

Who Wants to Be a Beggar?

Many of us have a bitter distaste for considering ourselves beggars. Earning favor, making restitution, and being a deserving recipient are considered honorable goals. When it comes to receiving Christ's righteousness in exchange for our sin, we are handicapped by such ambition. Brennan Manning has written, "We are all, equally, privileged but unentitled beggars at the door of God's mercy!"[10]

Once we gladly acknowledge our inability to produce and perform to earn God's gifts, we will be confronted with our own inescapable need for mercy. Finding ourselves as beggars grants us the advantage of being dependent and willing to receive God's mercy. The magnitude of what we receive from him is too great for us to calculate repayment. We are smitten by the severe mercy of the One at whose door we've been begging, and our natural impulse is to follow him! To go where he goes, so we don't lose sight of him.

Following Christ is not a sterile form of making restitution, it is glad friendship, awe-filled worship, a pleasure, and a delight. When Christ is our delight, his desires become our own, and he is honored (see Psalm 37:4).

We honor him by asking, because our requests confirm we believe he is able.

We honor him by receiving, because we acknowledge he knows best what to give.

We honor him by our grateful longing to be with him because he is our delight.

Defiant Beggars as Grateful Disciples

The disguised gifts of the blind beggar are ours, as well. Usually we don't want them. We don't want to be needy, dependent, or unable to repay. We are sometimes embarrassed to receive. We think people with remarkable faith ought to "do better." But if we acknowledge that our need and dependence are gifts with which we can honor God, he will open our eyes to see that they are not shameful disadvantages, but holy advantages that drive us to him.

Sometimes we'll be shushed for relying so heavily on Christ. Sometimes we'll scold ourselves for being so needy. But if we offer these gifts to Christ, we receive from him the uncommon freedom that comes from asking him to provide for our most obvious needs.

Remarkable faith defies silencing, and calls out to Jesus for the help needed. With arms outstretched to Jesus, defiant faith gladly receives vision, life, and the irresistible desire to follow him. As we delight in him, he transforms affliction into affection and makes beggars into disciples.

—

Lord,

You are a compassionate, powerful king. Help me trust what I have learned of you, though I have not seen you with my eyes.

I confess I let circumstances cloud my vision of who you are. Pain and doubts blind me. Give me the courage to cry out for you, even when others would ridicule and silence me.

Thank you that your command to helpless, blind sinners is to simply receive. With my hands empty and open, I thank you for whatever you give.

And, Father, when I finally catch a glimpse of who you are, when you transform my need into irrepressible affection, nothing will be able to suppress my worship or keep me from following you.

Flagrant Faith

A Forgiven Woman Honors Jesus

When one of the Pharisees invited Jesus to have dinner with him, he went to the Pharisee's house and reclined at the table. A woman in that town who lived a sinful life learned that Jesus was eating at the Pharisee's house, so she came there with an alabaster jar of perfume. As she stood behind him at his feet weeping, she began to wet his feet with her tears. Then she wiped them with her hair, kissed them and poured perfume on them.

When the Pharisee who had invited him saw this, he said to himself, "If this man were a prophet, he would know who is touching him and what kind of woman she is—that she is a sinner."

Jesus answered him, "Simon, I have something to tell you."

"Tell me, teacher," he said.

"Two people owed money to a certain moneylender. One owed him five hundred denarii, and the other fifty. Neither of them had the money to pay him back, so he forgave the debts of both. Now which of them will love him more?"

Simon replied, "I suppose the one who had the bigger debt forgiven."

"You have judged correctly," Jesus said.

Then he turned toward the woman and said to Simon, "Do you see this woman? I came into your house. You did not give me any water for my feet, but she wet my feet with her tears and wiped them with her hair. You did not give me a kiss, but this woman, from the time I entered, has not stopped kissing my feet. You did not put oil on my head, but she has poured perfume on my feet. Therefore, I tell you, her many sins have been forgiven—as her great love has shown. But whoever has been forgiven little loves little."

Then Jesus said to her, "Your sins are forgiven."

The other guests began to say among themselves, "Who is this who even forgives sins?"

Jesus said to the woman, "Your faith has saved you; go in peace."

—Luke 7:36–50

She hadn't taken a customer in days so it was easy to dismiss her servants early. As soon as the last one was out the door, she lowered the inside lock and it clicked into place. Hurry and anticipation caused beads of sweat on her forehead and she could feel trickles down her back. She flung back the heavy curtain that concealed treasures she'd taken as payment and began rifling through them. A gold bracelet so heavy she'd never worn it. A pile of earrings, some paired, some mismatched, several boasting a jewel.

She lifted a delicate silver chain, dangled it over her open hand, and then let it drip, link by tiny link, into her palm. Too fine for daily wear and too valuable to trade, it was perfect. She poured it out of her palm onto the table and searched for its precious pendant.

She hoisted a shallow crate from behind the curtain and onto the table. Tiny jars of oils and perfumes clinked against each other. Most were no bigger than her thumb. Rummaging through them, she fingered the flattened tops and various shapes of rounded bodies. *Where is it?* In the early days she'd accepted as many of these as were offered, but since they were so common, she had been unable to sell or trade them for much.

She'd used many of them to gladden her face and

revive her empty heart. But soon she discovered that pretty jars and fragrant oils were useless for both.

Finally, she dredged up a soft leather pouch from under the collection. Withdrawing an exquisite jar, she held it to her flaming lamp. Like the others it was carved from alabaster, but this tiny vessel was nearly translucent. She tipped it in front of the lamp and saw the precious liquid angle toward the top. Encircling its neck were two delicately carved parallel ropes. Between them, a band of granular sapphires glimmered with a warning: snap the neck, spill the contents, sacrifice the value.

Attaching the chain to the neck of the alabaster jar, she placed it over her head. She pinned her long hair into a roll at the base of her neck and covered her head with a lovely and modest scarf. It was a new look for her. Thick black hair uncovered and rolling down her back had been her signature, a clear indication to fishermen, merchants, and travelers of the service they might receive inside her house. She picked up the bronze hand mirror she had traded from a wealthy Egyptian traveler and surveyed her appearance. With her locks rolled up and pinned neatly in place, she hardly recognized herself. She smiled.

The perfume fastened around her neck was strong

and the jar so thin that warmth from her body had already begun to liberate the fragrance and cover the stench of her trade. Men had always disgusted her, but they had money, and money meant survival. The "arrangement," as her first client had called it, began in the market where he saw her bartering with a baker. In exchange for a fresh loaf of bread she had offered the baker a handful of almonds she'd scrounged from a spilled basket. The baker was unmoved. "No!" he spat. "Take your dirty wares off my table." Hungry and defeated, she left. Near the end of the market street the stranger caught up to her, handed her the loaf she couldn't buy, and offered her a proposition. Their needs intersected. She could escape starvation, he would provide. Weak with hunger and sickened by her options, a life sentence of either poverty or prostitution, she accepted his offer and bought her freedom with the only thing she owned—her "used-up" body. Her husband had said so when he cast her out like a dirty rag sopped with someone else's sin. He had been mean, inattentive, and demanding, and when she finally refused his sexual advances, he divorced her. To survive, she sold herself.

The alabaster jar and its perfume were a comfort to her. It covered the odor of men with sour wine and permeated the air with the clean aroma of forgiveness. It was everything she had wanted to be—lovely, cherished, and unused. It would be the perfect gift for the One who had looked at her with compassion, as a person to be valued and not a thing to be handled. She knew exactly where to find him, if she hurried.

She stepped into the courtyard and the idle chatter of every man standing there stopped, a silent reminder that she was not welcome. The house with its spacious courtyard and arched entry boasted of propriety. It was almost as well known as her house but for vastly different reasons. This was the home of Simon the Pharisee, a civil and religious pillar, a lawmaker, law keeper, everything she wasn't. Even with her hair pulled up and her head properly covered, every man in the courtyard recognized her. As she expected, a man dressed in full religious regalia held out an arm to halt her at the gate. Being cautious not to touch her, he urged the gathering men to pass in front of her and go on in.

"It's a public gathering," she said.

"It's a private house."

"None of these live here." She motioned to those stepping up the veranda in front of her.

"None of these are you."

Another man joined the one opposing her. "She may prove to be...a useful guest." He feigned a coy smile and winked. They turned their backs to her, murmured together, and nodded. Sweeping their hands toward the stairs, they extended a false welcome and allowed her to pass. Walking through the courtyard toward the threshold of the house, she felt the stares. She stepped up into the large open room where Simon and all his honored guests reclined together ready to eat.

The table was set low to the ground with all the trappings of a formal banquet. Each of the honored guests leaned on his elbow, feet extended away from the lovely setting, awaiting the start of the meal. Others stood crowded around the reclining guests. Aromas of roasted lamb, seasoned onions, and bread wafted through the room. In their rabbinical musings, the men diced up religious laws and scraped them off in stingy portions, dishing out made-up rules and congratulating one another for keeping them.

She shouldered her way through the crowded room, and men gasped at her flagrant disregard for social and religious propriety. They were there to consume any wisdom left on the table by these proud leaders. Perhaps by proximity they might attain such a worthy status as "friend of a Pharisee."

She had not come to pick through leftover theology. She had already heard and believed the One she had come to honor. She was changed.

Every man she passed on her way to him nearly jumped out of her way. If she had been the only woman in the room she would have been a distraction, but she wasn't just any woman. They knew who she was. Or at least what she had been. She was a blight on their gathering. Her shadow soiled whatever it fell upon. Those she passed dusted the filth of her shadow off their robes. They writhed with silent agitation and panic. One man spat in her direction and left the room. Several followed him.

Simon, the host, looked to his servants in a panic and urged them to begin the meal.

Disgust was written on every face but one, and now she stood directly behind him. He was at ease. Neither her bold journey around the outskirts of the room, nor the host's worried squirming had affected his unmistakable calm. Jesus. Here he was! While everyone shivered at her presence, Jesus remained unshaken.

Thankfulness pounded in her chest demanding to be released. Here was the One who'd declared himself not only a friend to sinners, but the forgiver of sins. She had wanted nothing more than to be freed from the reputation, duties, and succession of cruel masters. Utter freedom didn't seem possible, but it was. Everything she'd heard about him, the words he'd spoken, everything that galled the religious leaders drew her to him. Gladness welled in her eyes, and she willed it not to spill out.

As she stood behind him near his extended feet, his closeness and kindness overcame her. She suppressed an explosive sob, but it escaped in what sounded like a cough. She clapped her hand over her mouth. Holding back grateful tears could not restore dignity, so she let them flow. A shower of tears dripped from her nose and chin. The salty offering seeped into her mouth as she gasped for a calming breath. Finally, they landed on Jesus' feet. When her tears cut a trail through the dust on his feet, she noticed Simon had not extended the courtesy of washing them. Simon had no idea whom he was hosting. A teacher, perhaps. A prophet, maybe. But the merciful Son of God? He had no idea.

Instinctively she went to her knees to clean up the

mess she had made on the One she had hoped to honor. She removed the scarf from her head, pulled the long pin from her knotted hair, and let it fall to the side of her neck. Ignoring the collective gasp at her blatant immodesty, she wiped her shower of tears with her hair, smearing the wet dust in an effort to clean and dry his feet. It was the most pathetic service she'd ever rendered.

Jesus did not scold her. Neither did Simon. She peered through the hair hanging in her eyes. Every eye was on Jesus. Simon and all his dinner guests had stopped eating. The servants stood frozen, as if breathing would fuel the inevitable eruption.

Jesus continued to eat. He made no gesture, no movement but to enjoy the meal.

She looked down again at his precious feet, which had come so far to bring such good news and which she had muddied in an effort to clean. Bending farther forward she pressed her lips to his feet and began kissing them. What precious news they had brought to her: forgiveness, a fresh start, new life. *Oh, Jesus. Thank you.* She could not give the words volume. Her throat was still clogged with sobs. She was a mess of a spectacle, and his presence and acceptance removed every shred of shame. Clusters of men began filing out of the house, voicing embarrassment and disgust that the honored guest tolerated her behavior, cursing as they left the gathering.

She raised her head again and reached inside her cloak to do what she had planned to do. Grasping the beautiful pendant of perfume, she pulled the chain over her head. She snapped the delicate neck and watched the sapphires scatter over the floor. Grains of beauty mixed with common sand as she ignored the sapphires' warning and sacrificed the value to Jesus. The aroma rolled out as she poured the perfume on his feet.

She wanted to explain, but the thick fragrance stirred up a cough, and she could not. It trickled over his feet, onto the stone floor, and settled in the cracks where the sapphires had fallen. Again, she wiped his feet with the ends of her now matted hair. She kissed his feet again and again. *Thank you. Thank you.*

The room was dreadfully silent except for the squirming guests who remained. A servant entered, saw her hunched at Jesus' feet, and was so startled that he dropped his platter. Simon flinched and slammed his hand down on the table as if demanding a stop to it all.

In response, Jesus spoke: "Simon, I have something to tell you." His voice was calm.

Her stomach churned with anticipation. She kissed his feet again because his voice invoked more gratitude. Raising her head she looked at Simon. Muted rage distorted his face.

"Say it, Teacher."

Thankful for the veil of her hair, she bowed and touched her lips to Jesus' feet again as she listened. Curiosity quieted her weeping, but the tears still came.

"Two men owed money to a lender," Jesus said. "One owed him ten times what the other owed, but neither of them had anything to pay him back, so he canceled the debts of both. Which of them do you think would love him more?" Jesus looked up from his food and waited for Simon's answer.

Her tears came like rain now as he expressed her sin in financial terms. She had judged correctly. Not only had he forgiven her and canceled her debt, he knew her love for him. He shifted his weight, and she could tell Jesus was looking at her.

"Simon, do you see this woman?"

Simon was silent. Her presence was inescapable. How could he not?

He continued. "I entered your house and you didn't extend the honor of washing my feet. This woman had no water so she gave me an abundance of tears. You didn't see fit to lend me a towel but she has exposed her long hair, and extended a common courtesy to me."

She looked at his feet, the tops were wiped but muddied, far from clean, and still he commended her. She bowed to kiss them again.

"You have not greeted me with a kiss to affirm our commonalities in God, but nearly from the time I came in she has not stopped kissing my feet. And you did not anoint my head even with common olive oil, but she has anointed my feet with this expensive perfume."

The fragile jar lay broken and emptied. Used up, but not for nothing.

"Listen, Simon. Her sins, which are many, are forgiven. That is why she loves so much."

She tried to affirm it. *I do love you! So much!* But the choking sobs constricted her throat again.

"But, Simon, the one who is forgiven little, loves little."

Jesus pushed himself up from the table, crossed his legs, and sat on the floor facing her. "Your sins are forgiven," he said.

She smiled and nodded. *I know.*

"Your faith has saved you; go in peace."

The room erupted with grumbling and whispered curses. "How does this man presume to forgive sin? Who does he think he is?"

She picked up the broken jar, retrieved her scarf and hairpin, and bowed her head in gratitude once more. Broken by forgiveness, she had spilled wordless worship, and he had accepted her gift. She was forgiven and free.

Honorable Interruption

She knelt before Jesus as one of the most unlikely examples of faith we see in the gospels. Her hair was as muddied as her reputation. Everyone knew who she was. With such a sullied history, the religious leaders were sure to avoid her. She was the kind of woman you didn't want walking with you to the well, or in the market, lest you be associated with her ways.

When Jesus quantified her sin, he said they were many. Though everyone listening to Jesus was carrying a debt of sin, Jesus implied she was ten times the sinner any of the rest of them were.

She was a woman beaten and bruised by a cruel master called sin. Sin brings decay, destruction, and the earned wage of death (see Romans 6:23). Whatever she spent to free herself only drove her deeper in, and she had nothing with which to repay. She had no reason to believe she deserved to have her debt canceled. Working her way out was at best a wearisome prospect and at worst, impossible. But a woman wearied by working to repay an insurmountable sin debt is anxious and ready for rescue.

Perhaps on the hillsides of Galilee she heard Jesus pray aloud and thank God for revealing truth to little children. Perhaps she'd stuck around just long enough to hear his invitation, "Come to me all you who are weary and burdened, and I will give you rest" (Matthew 11:28).

It was the truth that would set her free. Jesus himself freely offered forgiveness—the cancellation of her debt. What he offered was all she needed, and she believed he told the truth. With that, the transaction was complete. He gave her rest from her striving, canceled the debt she'd racked up, paid her bill, satisfied her creditors, and gave her a new identity. So when old creditors attempted to shame her and collect what she no longer owed, she knew, "The debt is paid, and that woman is no longer here" (see Galatians 2:20). She had no reason to fear repayment because her debt was gone.

What does the rescued woman feel for the one who rescued her from such an impossibility? Much love. Her response is worship. Spending her expensive perfume on Jesus didn't rectify a transaction or reconcile her account. Lavishing honor facilitated a relationship, fellowship, friendship. For Jesus she will go where she is not welcome, interrupt in order to honor, weep without apology, and be thought a messy fool to worship without reserve.

Impossible Debts Paid

We each rack up sin debt in a myriad of ways, but we're born into it first. We are sinners, debtors from birth (see Romans 5:12). We plunge ourselves further into debt when we rebel against the boundaries meant to keep us safe or rationalize our reasons for going out of bounds. Sin holds out temporary happiness and delight for some, and for others, it dangles the prospect of survival. Sin may be the only path that appears clearly before us, and so we walk it, plunging headlong into slow and reasonable self-destruction. We think we are working ourselves out of a mess. But sin is always a liar.

Jesus always tells the truth. He is the Way, the Truth, and the Life (see John 14:6). He will cancel insurmountable debt if we'll only recognize the depth of it, admit we are incapable of reconciling our own account, and believe he has the authority to pay it off, no matter how large (see Romans 4:21–24).

Knowing we have been rescued by Christ from a debt we will never have to repay, and loving him because of it, is the starting point, the motivation, and the reward of worship. In other words, "We love him because he first loved us" (1 John 4:19). Although worship is sometimes messy or even embarrassing for others to watch, it is undeniable evidence of bare-faced, conspicuous, flagrant faith.

Forgiveness Leads to Worship

For many of us, even a partial list of sin and failure that hangs around in the back of the mind is enough to keep us from worshipping God wholeheartedly. After all, if he only knew what kind of person is worshipping him…He does know. He knows more of our failures than we do ourselves. He knows if our sins amount to ten or one hundred or one thousand times as much as that person sitting next to us. It feels embarrassing to ask for that much. But when we humbly ask him to forgive, to pay off that insurmountable debt, he will. His divine generosity stirs up genuine affection and love for Christ. That love is sometimes demonstrated with tears, raised hands, a song, or a work of art. The person who has not been forgiven and freed cannot understand such personal expressions of worship. Jesus does. He welcomes and accepts the remarkable worship that erupts from the heart of flagrant faith.

Lord Jesus,

I owe a dreadful debt I don't like to recall and can't afford to repay. But on the cross you canceled it. You stamped it in blood: paid in full.

You have not merely set me at a zero balance, you've also lavished me with the riches of your grace, gifted me with your Spirit, and dressed me in your perfection. The duty I once felt has now become an irrepressible pleasure. I love and worship you.

Lord, let me worship without shame, restraint, or reserve. Free me to worship, like this woman, with flagrant faith.

Remarkable Faith in Disguise

Some of us have grown up with the notion that to be acceptable in God's eyes we needed to do something really big. Sunday school lessons and children's Bibles left us in wide-eyed wonder over the ark-builders, sea-crossers, and giant-slayers. We grew up genuinely wanting to live a God-pleasing life.

School and family, work and commitments seem to prevent us from performing what might be considered ark-building, sea-crossing acts of faith. Some days, and for some seasons, it has been difficult to serve in the local church regularly because of all the demands placed on us. It might cause us to wonder if, despite all our hurried striving, our faith might be second-rate, or at worst, nonexistent. We feel our faith is unremarkable.

But remarkable faith is often grown in the broken soil of desperation. Theologian and Bible teacher H. A. Ironside wrote, "God is looking for broken men who have judged themselves in the light of the cross of Christ. When He wants anything done, He takes up men who have come to the end of themselves, whose confidence is not in themselves, but in God."

Perhaps we have inadvertently turned our eyes upon the ark-builders and giant-slayers, instead of turning our eyes upon God, who empowers every single act of faith, regardless of its impact or visibility.

As a result we have become accustomed to thinking remarkable faith in God looks one way. A steady stream of bumper sticker inspiration, coffee mug quotes, and social media memes have been created to inspire and encourage us to demonstrate faith that way. We've heard of "strong faith" and the kind that helps us "take a leap of faith," or "get out of the boat." Faith is sometimes talked about as though it's the little "oomph" that helps a Christian "get back on the horse" or "pull yourself up by the bootstraps." "Let your faith be stronger than your fears," the bumper stickers tell us.

The faith we see demonstrated in these gospel stories, however, is faith that is acutely aware of desperate, impossible need. The bumper sticker inspiration doesn't mention that. We might resign ourselves to the belief that our constant need for him means our faith is weak. Nothing could be further from the truth!

To Love Honor and Need

In his book *Desiring God*, John Piper gives this memorable analogy of how Christ is honored when we acknowledge our ongoing need for him:

> Suppose you are totally paralyzed and can do nothing for yourself but talk. And suppose a strong and reliable friend promised to live with you and do whatever you needed done. How could you glorify your friend if a stranger came to see you? Would you glorify his generosity and strength by trying to get out of bed and carry him?
>
> No! You would say, "Friend, please come lift me up, and would you put a pillow behind me so I can look at my guest. And would you please put my glasses on for me?" And so your visitor would learn from your requests that you are helpless and that

your friend is strong and kind. You glorify your friend by needing him and asking him for help and counting on him.[11]

Jesus is that friend. We honor him by acknowledging our need for him, over and over and over. God is not annoyed with our neediness. Instead, he is glorified by dependence as we pray—even as we cry out and scream to him—with repentance and requests. "Prayer humbles us as needy and exalts God as wealthy."[12]

In the disappointment of our own inability, our merciful God has made a way for us to honor him! So let us not be ashamed of all the ways in which we need him. We need him more than we can fathom. We need him to rescue us from addictions and ingrained patterns of sinful behavior. We need him to deliver us from a chronic reliance on our own resources and intelligence. We even need him to save us from the destructive nature of pride and self-superiority when we've done well. We can honor him by our dependence no matter which direction we turn.

"If dependence on God is the objective, then weakness is an advantage."[13] It readies us to receive. This is why we can say with the apostle Paul, "Therefore I will boast all the more gladly about my weaknesses, so that Christ's power may rest on me" (2 Corinthians 12:9).

Earning a Wage versus Receiving a Gift

The idea of unabashed, openhanded receiving does not comport with our Western Christian work ethic. It is difficult to untangle the cultural work ethic from the gospel of Jesus. In Genesis we have the mandate to work the garden. In Proverbs we have warnings about laziness, and in the New Testament we have Paul urging us that in whatever we do we ought to "work at it with all your heart as working for the Lord" (Colossians 3:23).

We know service to God is good, right, and necessary. We've read "we are God's handiwork, created in Christ Jesus to do good works, which God prepared in advance for us to do" (Ephesians 2:10).

The problem begins when "the work he has planned for us" becomes a currency for us to earn his favor. When it becomes a transaction—a way to get what we want from God—it becomes poison to faith in Jesus. Earning is the opposite of the gospel of grace. We've earned a huge sin debt, and when you've earned something big, you get paid big wages. In this case, "the wages of sin is death" (Romans 6:23). While we were still racking up a debt of sin, God sent Jesus to pay it off. Instead of you and me getting paid the wage of death for what we've earned, Jesus was paid.

Normally when someone gets your pay it's a maddening mistake. In this case, it is good news. Nothing we could do enables our escape from that impending pay date with eternal death. We earned it, and Jesus got paid with the consequences of our innumerable sins, our continual offenses to the God who created and loved us. Jesus rescued us and traded places with you and me.

Not That Bad

We want to think, "I'm not that bad, I don't really need Jesus." If we think we don't need Jesus, we've dishonored him by our lack of faith. If we do not, like these gospel examples of remarkable faith, admit our desperation, pain, fatigue, hopelessness, disability, soul poverty, loneliness, and sin, we are saying we aren't that bad, and Jesus is not that honorable.

When we admit we lack anything that could earn God's favor, we are finally free to receive what Jesus gives in exchange for our sin—grace, God's undeserved love, favor, and righteousness. Grace can't be earned. It is a scandalous gift.

Grace permits us to come (nay, demands that we come) as empty sinners to be blessed, empty of right feelings, good character, and satisfactory record, with nothing to commend ourselves but our deep need, fully and frankly acknowledged. Then grace, being what it is, is drawn by the need to satisfy it just as water is drawn to depth that it might fill it.

This means that when at last we are content to find no merit nor procuring cause in ourselves, and are willing to admit the full extent of our sinfulness, then there is no limit to what God will do for the poor that look to Him in their nothingness. If what we receive from God is dependent, even to a small extent, on what we are or do, then the most we can expect is but an intermittent trickle of blessing.[14]

Jesus took away our sin, yes, but he did not leave a void in our spiritual account. He credited his righteousness to us! His record of sinless perfection has been given to us who admit our need for him. It was a divine cut and paste, as if he cut out his perfect record and pasted it to my account and yours.

When we recognize our inability to earn fellowship and favor with God and realize we must simply receive it as a gift of grace, this divine exchange—Jesus' righteous cut and paste—is exceedingly good news!

A Glorious Upward Spiral—Love, Obedience, Faith

In centuries past when prayer-fueled revivals sprang to life, Christians with a fresh understanding of the grace of God claimed to have been "seized with the power of a great affection." This antique language is still an accurate description of a believing heart wooed by a gracious Savior. In modern-day language we call it "worship."

Worship is the result—the reflex—of the person wowed by the grace of God and gripped with affection for the Almighty. How do we thank the One who has rescued us from death and lavished grace?

As we speak with him in prayer recounting all the ways he loved us, we might just sit up midsentence and suddenly say, "I'd like to do something for you Jesus, but I don't know what."

"If you love me, you will obey my commands," would be Jesus' response. It's why Jesus said the first and greatest commandment is to love God. Out of our genuine love flows delightful obedience. When we see glimpses of his activity in our long obedience, in the difficulties that drive us to him, we are overcome with love and worship. It only serves to make us love him more. From love flows obedience, and he shows himself again . . . which makes us love him. It is a blessed cycle begun by his drastic rescue, his scandalous grace, and it continues infinitely with affectionate worship.

It is an affection we can feel for the One who feels such affection for us that he initiated and completed this great exchange.

Portraits of the Gospel

Each of these stories of faith is a portrait of the gospel of Jesus Christ. Their impossible needs drove them to

Jesus. They pointed to nothing they had done to earn his favor. They had nothing to lose. With humiliating honesty they presented their needs to him. Some screamed, as in the case of the distant and defiant. Some said nothing, as in the case of the flagrant worshipper and the helpless paralytic. Some were quite articulate, as were the unworthy centurion and the panicked mother of the demon-possessed girl. The weak and suffering tell Jesus the whole broken story.

These individuals were real humans. Brennan Manning might have called them "ragamuffins." They were weak, unable, and unworthy. Instead of keeping them from Jesus, their afflictions drove them to him. They trusted that his touch, or his mere word, would be superior to any solution they'd already tried. They were willing to receive whatever he gave simply because he is Jesus. Each allowed grace to transform their inadequacies into irrepressible affection and worship.

Jesus took note of their faith, remarked and even marveled about it. After he saves, he tells them to go home, get up, go in peace, go your way. God gets the glory. The faithful get the joy of going to tell others about him.

Will He Find Faith?

Remarkable faith is not an archaic memory. It is a present reality. Will Jesus find faith when he comes again? Yes, he will. He will find it in the weak who beg for his help in merely believing. He will find it in the helpless without a single visible good deed to point to as evidence of faith. He will find it in the unworthy who recognize Christ's authority to declare them worthy. He will find it in the suffering who have clung to him through the pain. He will find it in the distant outcast who has accepted his welcome and worshipped because of it. He will find it in the panicked who have been deluded by false gods and delivered by the True God. He will find it in the defiant who have thrown off undue expectations to follow Christ. He will find it in the flagrant worshipper who is not too embarrassed to love him.

If you and I have admitted our sin, asked him to save us and believed that he will, then he will certainly find remarkable faith in you and me.

Acknowledgments

A million thanks to...

Kurt for your patience and support over a very long time.

My Prayer Team, for praying with me and for me and this project over the years.

Ken Gire for teaching me that writing is not a coward's profession and that if your king commissions you to "run behind the lines and tell the stories," then you must.

To Cindy for your honesty about needed improvements, your inestimable help in crafting the proposal, and your ongoing enthusiasm.

To Dan Balow for being my patient tour guide and translator in a foreign country called "publishing."

To Adrienne and the FaithWords team for your enthusiasm and for taking a chance on me.

To Sara for wading through first drafts and being so honest with your feedback and generous with your time.

To friends and family too numerous to list who listened politely as I blathered on about proposals, word count, story structure, agents, and publishing. You have been so kind and patient with me. Thanks for being my continual cheerleaders.

To the Chief Hopers and all the Hope*Writers, for being a community committed to spreading hope.

I'm so grateful for each of you who has pointed me to Jesus. He writes the best stories!

Notes

1. Philip Yancey, *The Jesus I Never Knew* (Grand Rapids, MI: Zondervan, 1995), 95.
2. Howard Hendricks, *Living by the Book* (Chicago: Moody Publishers, 2007), 107.
3. Jim Cymbala, *Fresh Wind, Fresh Fire* (Grand Rapids, MI: Zondervan, 1997), 19.
4. Brennan Manning, *The Ragamuffin Gospel* (Colorado Springs, CO: WaterBrook Multnomah, 2005), 28.
5. Also rendered: be of good cheer (King James Version); Take heart (NIV); Be encouraged (New Living Translation); Have courage, son (Holman Christian Standard Bible); Cheer up (The Living Bible, The Message).
6. Darrell L. Bock, *Luke 1:1–9:50, Baker Exegetical Commentary on the New Testament* (Grand Rapids, MI: Baker Books, 1996), 644.
7. Roy Hession, *We Would See Jesus* (Fort Washington, PA: CLC Ministries, 2005), 9.
8. Darrell L. Bock, *Luke 9:51–24:53, Baker Exegetical Commentary on the New Testament* (Grand Rapids, MI: Baker Books, 1996), 1406.

9. John Koessler, *The Radical Pursuit of Rest* (Downers Grove, IL: InterVarsity Press, 2016), 98.

10. Manning, *The Ragamuffin Gospel*, 26.

11. John Piper, *Desiring God: Meditations of a Christian Hedonist* (Sisters, Oregon: Multnomah Books, 1996), 138.

12. Ibid.

13. Alistair Begg's Truth for Life Twitter feed, tweet posted May 11, 2015: https://twitter.com/truthforlife/status/59776385565002 1376.

14. Hession, *We Would See Jesus*, 9–10.